CW01236682

Other Works by Didymus. D. Thomas

The Islamic Pope

The Perfect Parables

The Anglican Apostasy

DIDYMUS D. THOMAS

The Bloody Religion of Peace

authorHOUSE

AuthorHouse™ UK
1663 Liberty Drive
Bloomington, IN 47403 USA
www.authorhouse.co.uk
Phone: 0800.197.4150

© 2018 Didymus Thomas. All rights reserved.

No part of this book may be reproduced, stored in a retrieval system, or transmitted by any means without the written permission of the author.

Published by AuthorHouse 02/21/2018

ISBN: 978-1-5462-8518-2 (sc)
ISBN: 978-1-5462-8519-9 (hc)
ISBN: 978-1-5462-8517-5 (e)

Print information available on the last page.

Any people depicted in stock imagery provided by Thinkstock are models, and such images are being used for illustrative purposes only.
Certain stock imagery © Thinkstock.

This book is printed on acid-free paper.

Because of the dynamic nature of the Internet, any web addresses or links contained in this book may have changed since publication and may no longer be valid. The views expressed in this work are solely those of the author and do not necessarily reflect the views of the publisher, and the publisher hereby disclaims any responsibility for them.

Islamic scholarship divides the world in to two spheres of influence; the House of Islam (dar al-Islam) and the House of War (dar al-harb). Since Islam means a servile submission, the House of Islam includes those nations that have submitted or surrendered to Islamic rule, which is to say; all those nations ruled by sharia law. The remainder of the world, which has not accepted sharia law, is patently not in a state of submission but remains in a state of war and rebellion against Allah. It is and always has been, incumbent on dar al-Islam to wage war upon Dar al-Harb, until such time that all nations bend the knee to Allah and are sharia compliant. Islam's message to the non-Muslim world is the same today as in Muhammad's day; submit or be slain!

Author contact details:

PO BOX 22
1857 WEST FOURTH AVE
VANCOUVER BC
V6J 1M4

Dedication

In a plea for truth and freedom, and in fervent protest against the misinformation and propaganda that enslave the mind and foment evil, this book is dedicated and devoted to the coming peace of Jerusalem and to every victim of terrorism

Preface

The current insurgence of Islam is not exactly a new phenomenon. Ever since Muhammad met his demise in the seventh century, Muslims have been fanning out across the globe. What is different today is that Islam is surging throughout the world generally, and Europe specifically. The methodology driving the increased momentum is primarily the subterfuge of the nefarious Muslim Brotherhood, which is rightly categorised as a terrorist organisation by some countries—but sadly not by all. MB is supported and sponsored by a long list of scurrilous Arab nations who are filthy rich in black gold.

When Muslims first arrived in Europe, they did not rattle any cages or rock any boats; they merely melted in, almost unnoticed. At first it was just a gentle stream, but in the blink of an eye, the trickle became a flooding river. Muslims began pouring into countries and cities like there was no tomorrow. Governments became paralysed by the suddenness and the overwhelming numbers of so-called refugees and migrants. Many migrants entered Europe as a fox entering the henhouse. Millions of Muslims duped authorities about their status by pretending they were refugees, but in reality they were migrants. There is a clarion disparity between the two, and that is why many Muslims lied so eloquently. The United Nations clarifies the distinctness: "A refugee is forced to leave his country and a migrant chooses to leave their country." An unknown number of men deceived countless countries about their age by masquerading as teenagers. This produced catastrophic results, with men mixed with children. The total number of children raped, sodomised, and sexually assaulted will, through negligence and embarrassment, remain a secret statistic. This current avalanche of displaced people should not cause such a huge consternation for the comatose European leaders. They were warned by both Abu Bakr al-Baghdadi (ISIS) and Ayman Mohammad Zawahiri (al-Qaeda) at the end of 2014 and the start of 2015 about this deluge of foreigners. The warning was elevated to a threat, and now ten million mujahideen (soldiers) would come. As we glance out at the turbulent sea of souls, we have to confess that the threat is being realised. Their intimidation is proving profitable with nations holding their breath. It is clear that these hordes have no intention to integrate but every inclination to subjugate.

It was Winston Churchill who talked about Muslims in "mathematical" terms. He was referring to the Islamic agenda to obtain numerical superiority wherever they go. The Muslim birth rate is usually six times greater than the local populace. Mainland Europe is already experiencing the discomfort of this scenario. An example is found in a Somali man settled in Sweden who has four wives and twenty-three children—all being supported by state benefits. The goal of supremacy is paramount in ideological Islam. It is an imperative to infiltrate all areas of the host country, with the aim of increasing Muslim influence. Instead of contributing to the infrastructure of a nation, they do their level best to dismantle every democratic nut and bolt. There are two tsunamis on the horizon for which we should be prepared. The first is supremacy, and the second is sharia.

"Cursed is a most inauspicious place to be. How wretched it is that multitudes of Muslims have the offer of light but implausibly choose a black hole and darkness. God says, 'Let there be light,' but men preferred darkness."

– William Gladstone

Chapter One

Allah

"The totalitarian Islamist doctrine of Allah mandates the spread of Islam by all believers and submission to its laws even by non-believers. Not all Muslims practice this, but those who do represent a major threat to the free world."

- Hugh Fitzgerald.

The morning meetings in the White House were many things but they were never prosaic affairs. As the group stood silently in the Oval Room, preparing for prayer, they were suddenly conscious of the trio of resident witnesses. Three bronze busts of Winston Churchill, Abraham Lincoln and Dwight Eisenhower, who were never late and never missed a meeting; were watching and waiting. Today, would be different. The president of the United States of America, a rather reticent Christian; was asked something no-one else had done so before. "Mr. President, I have been considering the question of Allah and the Quran and the God of the Bible. Do you believe they are the same god?" After a silence that stretched longer than Pennsylvania Avenue, the president hesitatingly spoke and as he did the gathering was stunned into a sombre silence. Bush was not spoilt for choices – it could not be any easier. All eyes were fixed and focused on the president. Finally, George Bush gave his brief response; "I believe we all worship the same God – they just have different names." A pin could be heard dropping on the floor; several hearts missed a rhythmic beat and others glanced fleetingly around the room. The "Christian" president had to make a simple decision but predictably Bush blundered badly!

When Dave Hunt the author and apologist was alive, he was known to say, "The distance between Allah and God is incalculable and the difference between them is immeasurable." The fly in the ointment for Islam is that we read that Allah of the Quran has no son but the God of the Bible does have a Son. This leaves not just Muslim's but mankind in a precarious position. Each one of the estimated seven billion world population is compelled to make a choice. Which "god" will we choose or reject? If they possessed just one minor distinction they would still not be the same god. This statement is unequivocal. The litmus test in this matter is the author of the holy books – who wrote the Quran and who penned the Bible? There is an ardent activist who opposes the Islamisation of America. She was a Muslim in war torn Lebanon and used to read the Quran religiously and repeatedly in the cellar of her bombed building. She became disillusioned because no matter how often she read the book she always failed to find the author. Brigitte Gabriel was then persuaded to read the Bible and in an instant she confessed that instead of her finding the author, the writer found her. Miraculously, Gabriel was set free. Rather than being a slave to a lifeless god she had become a servant of the living God.

We have to appreciate that just because people have bought in to a faith or have been sold an ideology – it does not make it a legitimate religion. Not so long ago multitudes were fanatical followers of Fascism and others zealously committed to Communism but neither of these possessed a god or could be classified as a religion or faith. While Allah has become the proper name for the Muslim god and the Islamic "religion," Allah is not simply a name. The number of people who know and notice this matter is remarkably few. Allah goes beyond being a name to becoming a specific description which literally means "the god." In comparison to Christianity, Allah was originally no more a proper name for the Muslim god than the designated word "Almighty" is the only formal title for the Christian God. Muslims commonly and spuriously make the mistake of calling the two deities by the same name; god. This is a puerile problem that is easily overcome by comparing the god of the Quran against the God of the Bible.

The researcher, Dr. Labib, says, "...the differences between the two god's is inscrutable and irreconcilable..." Unfortunately, the conundrum which Labib failed to expunge and explain; is the fulcrum that differentiates them both. We mean of course, that God is alive and that Allah has never lived, except in the furtive imagination of his followers. Such a profundity so great is unimaginable – one billion Muslims praying five times a day and to whom? A non-existent "god." If we were to ask a Muslim if his prayers have ever been answered the reaction would be one of incredulity. Such a concept is nothing more than an alien notion to those indoctrinated by Islam.

The Arabic word for prayer is *Salah*, which is the second of the five pillars of Islam. Children are instructed how to pray from an early age. A toddler, named Salat, which interestingly also means prayer, was heard screaming out the only prayer she knew. Salat was laying on her back with her legs wide open. There were two heavy women holding her arms and legs and her father was kneeling between her thighs with a well-worn pair of scissors in his hand. He is about to perform an act of mutilation that Allah and the Quran mandate. There is nothing medicinal available, just an unclean rag and the stained scissors. The child's father took hold of the clitoris with his left finger and thumb and with the scissors clumsily cut his way through the flesh. The rag was insufficient and blood soon began to spread over the body and down the legs of the little girl. This atrocious act of Female Genital Mutilation (FGM) is unnecessary and provides no benefit for the child. All this trauma is for two reasons only. It is said to increase fidelity since there is now no satisfaction to be gained for the female and for the man, it allegedly enhances the perverted sexual pleasure he receives. No other religion on earth is as barbaric as "The Bloody Religion of Peace."

Unlike any other nominal "religion," Islam, as well as being a hybrid, is a wholly materialistic and corporeal contrivance. Everything about Allah and Islam is fundamentally self-centred. The focus of prayer and the object of pilgrimage to a black block of rock (Kabah) is infinitely egocentric. When you consider the birth and death of a Muslim, it is from the cradle to the grave a carnally driven existence. Contemplate for a moment and consider what is in the mind of a Muslim on his death bed. Uppermost in his thoughts are the possible rich rewards on offer, which is one of the reasons why Muslim's find dying has so much appeal; supposedly seventy two virgins for endless copulation, strings of pearls or boys for sodomy, self-satisfaction, sensual ambiance and self-indulgence are all supposedly waiting in wonder. Christine Williams of Jihad Watch crystallises the matter by reminding the reader that Islam has the unwanted distinction of being the only "religion" where territorial sovereignty is more desirable than spiritual sovereignty. Once again we are exposed to the obsessive traits that are to be found in the mindset of any materialistic Muslim.

The universal consensus is that not just one group of Muslims but every Muslim sect, who fervently deny that Allah was being worshipped at the Meccan Kabah, by Arab pagans, long before Muhammad marched on to the secular stage. When a Muslim is confronted with this fact, they invariably become acutely angry. Even if that anger reaches boiling point they still cannot escape from the historical record found in pre-Islamic antiquity. In one factual and creditable account by author G. J. O. Moshay; his book asks a pointed question, "Who is this Allah?" The conclusion he arrives at is that Allah was indubitably worshipped as a pagan god before the Kabah ever appeared on the sand-swept landscape. He goes on to say that the weight of evidence to support this is sufficient to re-sink the Titanic. The undeniable truth is that pagan Arabs were using the name Allah as the chief pagan god of their pantheon, the Kabah, with its exorbitant 360 idols of worship. The significance of the number is that every Arab house could have its very own god. Even Muhammad flirted with idolatry and this alarming fact is well recorded by al-Bukhari in the Hadith (al-Bukhari 7:407)

It is worth re-iterating that it is widely accepted the Arabic word for god is "ilah" and "al" is the Arabic word for "the." It is not difficult to see that if the "i" is dropped, as is common with other Arabic words of vocabulary, we are left with "Allah" or "the god." In the same way, for instance; the Biblical God has "Almighty" as a personal name, "Allah" is the designated name of the pre-Islamic god. This is established throughout the Quran and is also written in parallel literature such as the Hadith (words and deeds of Muhammad). Disconcertingly, at this time in Muhammad's town of Mecca, polytheism was prevalent with multitudinous idols being worshipped. Idolatry was eagerly accepted and practised before, during and after the rule of Muhammad. For instance, followers of the "moon god," would ritualistically and religiously bow down to worship Allah at the Kabah. This is the familiar square slice of black rock believed to be off a meteorite from heaven and which sits inside the House of Allah Mosque. Today, its appearance has barely changed and still retains its cuboid and blackened configuration, measuring some six hundred and twenty square feet. It is estimated that millions make pilgrimages or *hajj* to the Kabah; just to embrace the rock and even to actually kiss it! How incongruous is such a foolhardy and farfetched whim.

One of the most obstreperous apologetic voices in Islam today is Dr. Zakir Naik. He calls himself a medical practitioner but is more accurately a diffident doctor. The man has been discredited and disgraced by Islam Watch and others. This controversial "scholar," who has a theological achilles heel; denies that Muslims worship the Kabah. His pretentious explanation is that Muslims flock to the Kabah for "geographical reasons;" it being a central place. The very same year that Naik made that pubescent comment, in excess of 3,000,000 Muslims made hajj, as pilgrims to worship, touch and kiss the inanimate Kabah. This episode of flocking to the Kabah is an example of where the line is clearly drawn; it is what separates the two main monotheistic belief systems. Islam and Muslims cannot conceivably have a personal relationship with a black rock, or an unknown god named Allah. Conversely, we learn that Christians through Christ can have a living and loving relationship with God. Jesus said, "...If a man love me, he will keep my word: and my Father will love him." The love of the Creator God is infinite to those who love Him.

The "religion" of Islam, has from the outset, venerated a deity called "Allah." Many Muslims claim quite outlandishly that Allah was a pre-Islamic god. Since Christianity pre-dates Islam, the question arises was Allah the Biblical or a pagan god? Many Muslims have speculated on the origin of Allah and this has become a contentious bone on which to chew. If it can be proved that Allah was a pre-Islamic pagan deity then the plethora of denials will collapse like a house built on sand. Muslims and Islam insist on exploring the archaeological "footprint" to substantiate their claims that Allah is god. Whilst Muslims insist on hard evidence to prove a point; it is this very evidence that prevents them from making ends meet. The affirmation is incontrovertible and demonstrates decisively that the god, Allah, was a pagan deity. In fact, a capricious number of tribes referred to him as the "moon god" who was married to the sun goddess and the stars were their daughters. This is not a subject of academic analysis but rather an historically established edict. "The Cult of the Moon God" by Brian Wilson, unearths the unpopular belief that Islam is no more than a Cult. Wilson demolishes the argument that Islam is a religion and demonstrates that it was nothing more than a mediocre pagan cult. An apostate, Abdullah al-Abdullah, pours petrol on the fire when he affirms, "It is impossible to love Allah since he never loves us." We understand from reading Scripture that there are two strands of love in the Bible. Both *philio* (horizontal love) and *agape* (vertical love) are Greek words that translate as love. When perusing the Quran it soon becomes apparent that these God-given qualities are conspicuous by there absence. Countless surveys have taken place to determine the number of uses of the word love in the Quran. The work of Dr. William Walden eruditely leaves us in no doubt; "Since the Quran is so congested with hatred there is no room for any love."

In Muhammad's day worshippers would walk around "the rock" several times and worship Allah. Not a great deal has changed except that Muslims now bend and bow towards the Kabah five times a day to pray. The 40 foot high black idol attracts multitudes of Muslim pilgrims who repeat more or less what the first idolaters did. It is highly relevant to mention that at *Ramadan* (A month of fasting), the Muslim holy month cannot begin until the new crescent moon is seen with the naked eye. We all know that often perched on top of a church is a cross. This is a universal symbol that conveys the message, "Christ Crucified." In contrast, on the roof of a Mosque you will find attached not a cross but a minaret with a crescent moon and star. The tallest minaret in the world sits in Algeria and stretches to 265 metres! Historian Huda Islam believes, "the Muslim crescent moon and star symbols actually pre-dates Islam by at least a thousand years." This would fit in firmly with early Islam's recorded pre-occupation with the worship of Allah as the familiar "moon god."

The picture would be incomplete if we did not remind ourselves that whilst Allah was the 'primary' god he was by no means the only deity manifest in Mecca. It is essential to etch in our minds that his name, is antediluvian. There are copious chronicles that support this assertion and which may be readily available in two Arabic documents, "Sabacan Records" and the "Minaean Yemini" parchments. Furthermore, before the name Allah was conceived and born it first appeared and occurred as "Hallah." We can be confident that Hallah was being employed as early as five centuries before the inception of Allah and Islam. Perhaps, most convincing of all we find that Muhammad's father was named 'Abd-Allah' which means "Abdullah, the worshipper of Allah." This source is unequivocal and has been the mainstay of many conservative commentators. When we place Allah on the scales he is left wanting. The evidence weighs heavily in favour of a heathen deity and not a heavenly God.

When Muhammad proclaimed the creed, "There is no god but Allah," he was not attempting to present or perfect a new god. His pagan fellow countryman knew only too well that the divine name of their god has always been Allah. This name was familiar the length and breadth of Arabia and was on the lips of men even before pre-Muhammadan days. From the first rumour of his conception, the Arab heathen had sufficient cognizance to discern that out of the hundreds of choices, believed to be in excess of 360, Allah; was the consummate god. In fact, Muhammad's preaching would invariably point back to this fact, thus solidifying his assent and their approval. Although Allah was worshipped generally, Muhammad was still more prevalent and he wanted this position reversed at all costs. Discontentment grew and Muhammad soon became disgruntled by the impasse. He knew deep down that even he could not live with this scenario. Muhammad wanted his god to be worshipped exclusively and none but him. Paganism and his own tribe the Quraish, added to the tension, for they were nothing more than a cult that was devoted to a multiplicity of godless gods. For example, some elected to worship the acclaimed idol *al-Lat*, a sun goddess; who had an arresting white cube to rival the black one in the Kabah ALLAH.

In WWII, (1943-44), in the Pacific Ocean, there was a plane and a pilot that everyone feared. It was the "kamikaze pilot" who flew suicidal missions in to the Australian and American Fleets. In all, they sacrificed 2,500 planes and men and killed over 5,000 sailors. Each Pilot was a young man who believed that sacrificing his life for the Emperor and Japan was the highest acclamation, and the surest course of salvation. Contemporaneously, Allah and Sharia personifies the picture of the kamikaze and the Emperor. Suicide bombers today operate instilling the same degree of fear as the suicide pilot. The similarity extends beyond the physical comparison to that of a spiritual analogy.

It would be remiss if we did not state here that Allah's Muslims are disingenuous and more deceitful than any other people group. All those who sanction and support Sharia Islamic Law; have been unknowingly caught off guard. Instead of swallowing the truth they have choked on a lie. Since Sharia is obnoxious, Muslim's are judicious in what they reveal. You will not be told in conversation, "Slay them wherever you find them" (Quran 4:89). Muhammadan's do not appear to possess a conscience, so will deliberately discriminate and withhold any passage that is factious or contentious. Instead, the Muslim will quote the less harmful and more benign parts, such as the practice of prayer. The psychology of this is to make it appear as if unbelievers are detractors and are simply religious bigots, whose real issue is intolerance and Islamophobia; which is so ridiculous that it is preposterous.

There is scattered in outer space a phenomena such as a "Black Hole." The reason scientist's claim this name is because the gravitational pull is so immense that not even a speck of light escapes. In Islam there is also a black hole without light; which Allah has commonly called the "Quran." We have, supposedly, one billion Muslims in the world who believe they are free when in actual fact, they are in bondage. Sharia law is servitude to a set of abhorrent rules and regulations that are the very antipathy of freedom. Of all the things that Sharia lacks, the most glaring feature is liberty. Islam repudiates any religious freedom; even the freedom of conscience is ridiculed. Unknown to virtually every Muslim, a man or woman under Sharia cannot be blessed. It does not matter how much noise they make, for it is all futile. Someone who is cursed cannot possibly be blessed. Imagine the implications of such a view as that. William Gladstone wrote, "Cursed is a most inauspicious place to be. How wretched it is that multitudes of Muslims have the offer of light but implausibly choose a hole of darkness." Muslim's are lost inside a tunnel that tragically has no light at the end. The theologian Tozer, articulated in his book, "In the Pursuit of God," that "darkness can only produce darkness."

The "enemedia" makes the news accessible but unfortunately it feeds the public a diet that is far from nourishing. For a long time the elites and know-it-alls, like Prince Charles, Justin Welby, Sadiq Khan, Barak Hussein Obama and Hilary Clinton, have condemned religious persecution but all of them have been derelict in their duty when it comes to name the guilty perpetrators. The only mass persecution in our time is conducted in the name of Allah by the infamous Islam. In Syria a monastery was ransacked, the men beheaded and the nuns raped. A church in Iraq was levelled and this time the women were spared being raped because they were shot in the head instead. In a peaceful retirement home for elderly monks and nuns in the French foothills, another planned persecution occurred and they were all routinely slaughtered. During broad daylight in Germany, a Somalian asylum seeker went in to a care home and sodomised two elderly disabled residents and on the way out he killed an 87 year old wife for good measure. Astonishingly, not one of the above elites had the courage to condemn these crimes committed in the name of Allah. It is not difficult to know and name the religion executing this murderous persecution. There is only one so-called religion in this world that is so implacable! It is indubitably Islam, "The Bloody Religion of Peace."

If we travelled to the U.K. or U.S.A; it is possible to follow in the footsteps of a symbolic survey that lasted over a year. This entailed visiting every main Mosque and initiating some discussion. The outcome of this exercise was phenomenal. Each and every *imam, sheikh* or *cleric* (often sexual predators or perpertrators), had one defined common denominator. We would be forgiven for assuming that it was Allah but we would be sorely mistaken. What all of these "pious" people had in common is that they lied through their teeth. The coincidental constituent was *taqiyya* or lying. This is of course, consistent with the Quran (16:106) which provides a trap door, or a get out clause, for this objectionable practice of prevaricating. If

Allah blesses the use of lying it is highly conceivable that Allah also lies. In fact, when we scrutinise the Quran we unearth what Allah calls *makr*, or the best deceiver. We read, "...the Jews are deceptive, and Allah was deceptive, for Allah is the best of deceivers" (Surah 27.50). The exemplary expositor, Sam Shamoun, makes reference to over 50 narratives where Allah is caught equivocating and living up to his ignominious reputation as the one who lies.

When we turn from our domestic scene to the international stage we find a totally different personality. The first player we encounter is the red-faced Erdogan, who is addressing the religious heads of Egypt and during the delivery he does not pull any punches. The controversial Egyptian leader began by saying, "Mosques are Islamic Barracks. It is where the Mujahideen (soldiers) are trained for battle." If you move in the right circles, such as the Machiavellian Muslim Brotherhood or the pernicious CAIR (Council On Islamic Relations), you will be reminded that Mosques masquerade; they are not what they seem. The religiosity is a smokescreen for terrorism. We currently have a surplus of loose legislature relating to the inspection of Mosques but there is a desperate need of it being tightened. Consider, for example, the Mosque in Dakota (U.S.A.) and in Didsbury (U.K.). These are two of a plethora of contentious locations that have slipped through the scrutiny of the security net. They preach supremacy and promote sharia.

When one stops to consider the conniving conduct in the Islamic community, it must be of prodigious interest to any national security echelon, for all mosque's to be more stringently regulated. Those who step out of line could be cautioned or closed. Guilty members could be detained and deported. We have no doubt whatsoever that every mosque is conspiring against our democratic society. It is only in the "civilised" West that terrorist's are placated. Quite recently, 400 Jihadist's returned from the Syrian conflict, via the "revolving door" of the UK immigration services. How many terrorist's do we believe were detained? It was a contemptible 54 out of 400! Those who gained entry have not surprisingly gone AWOL and are unaccountable. As far as we know they are being fed, watered and housed courtesy of state benefits and tax payers hard earned money.

It is widely known that ISIS/IS use state benefits to fund their terror campaign and to purchase their return airfare via Turkey or Egypt. Sweden has the unenviable reputation of succumbing to this Islamic onlaught. She has capitulated and will be the first European country to commit national suicide. Of course, it is not alone: both Belgium and Germany are also sleep-walking in to oblivion with their leaders appeasing Islam with bundles of blank cheques.

We are told, "It is the law!" There is not one country in the world that does not have some law or other. In the U.S.A. Congress is having difficulty keeping up with the epidemic of new crimes. Each time there is another crime committed then a new law has to be created. At the moment the running total is over 4,450 crimes (in a decade) which theoretically ought to bring a similar number of laws but not so. The truth is America has lost count of the exact number of laws it once had. Its information now is built on speculation. In the U.K. it is rumoured that the nation is law-abiding, which is both historical and hysterical. Since the majority of current laws are blown on a breeze from Europe; calculating the exact total is as challenging as counting the stars in the Milky Way. Between 1994 and 2014 Brussels intimated that a sagacious 49,699 laws were passed between Britain and the mainland. Andrew Parker (MI5) professed; "the country does not need any more of these laws. It is not more laws that the nation needs but more law keeper's." Parker's comments remind us of those of the Bible where Jesus states, "Blessed are the peacemakers..." The United Nations has an international army of peacekeepers but to our faux pas they are failing. Thank God for peacekeepers but the requirement for peacemaker's far outweighs the alternative.

Now, names are very important and that is why parents often agonise over choosing the right name for their child. The choice of the name Allah (Arabic) is immensely important. As designated in this work on another occasion, the common term Allah is the accepted Islamic word for "god." It is as earlier espoused more than likely procured from the Arabic article "al-ilah," meaning "deity or god" which when added to al-lah produces "the god." The repetition here is essential. All Arab speakers since the dawn of pre-Islamic times have used Allah in the context of their solitary god.

In fact, Allah became the widely approved generic term for god. This title Allah was ratified by none other than Muhammad ibn Abdullah, and was eagerly embraced by all true Islamic believers. It is pertinent at this juncture to highlight the point, that although Allah was predominantly accepted before and after Muhammad, not everyone bowed down to worship him. For instance, the Christian community, were called to worship a deity known as, "The true and living God;" and its followers vehemently refused to submit to an obscure and arcane pagan deity. All that was loosely known at this time was that the word *Islam* ("submission") meant bending the knee to Allah's will and a Muslim is one who completely surrenders to their god. Allah, frequently figures in every facet of the Quran's Islamic ideology. He is said to be transcendant and is thought by his followers to be "infallible" and "unchangeable," writes Abdullah Aal Mahmud, the egregious scholar.

If anything is likely to make a Muslims blood boil it is this question over when did Allah first appear. The fact that Allah was devoted as the pre-Islamic god is without question. Although, over a billion Muslim's find that this truth sticks in their throat and is unpalatable, the truth remains unchangeable. The historical evidence is piled higher than the 1,256 foot sand dune named Seven (Sab'ah) sitting in the Namibia Desert. Author, Syed Mirza, states there is sufficient affirmation for the "Allah Debate" to be conclusive. He goes on to say there is irrefutable documentation that shows pagan Arabs worshipped Allah. These idolaters did not limit their worship to just one god. They also devoted themselves to the sun, moon, and stars. It must be said that not every pre-Islamic Arab referred to the moon-god in the same way. At this time there was a plurality of idols and Allah was just one of many. As time passed and god's fell in and out of fashion, it was Allah who was predominant in the long list of pagan gods. The Islamic pagan deity was eventually worshipped in the Kabah (Most sacred Muslim site) as one of the affray totalling hundreds. We would be remiss if we did not mention that at the outset Muslims were originally instructed to worship the following false eminent gods, al-lat-Uzza (Surah 53:19-20). If that is true, what on earth happened to these important gods? Where did they disappear to? How can they be invaluable one minute and insignificant the next? "Abrogation." It is that convenient Islamic law of abrogation again. One of the most popular Islamic doctrines is abrogation. It is used as white wash to cover over all that proceeded the abrogation. The three "daughters of Allah" are an acute case in point. They quite simply disappeared, were deleted or, abrogated from the sacred writings without the slightest deprecation.

Of course, we know from what King Solomon said; "There is nothing new under the sun," and this applies to the controversy associated with the name Allah, which has fuelled the polemicists row long before Muhammad ever emerged on earth. The argument has been simmering for countless centuries and it is fundamentally over this important issue as to whether Allah is the "true god" or, if he is the pagan, "moon god." There is a lot at stake and the answer will either make or break this simmering situation. Allah is the approbation of the standard Arabic word for god and all Muslims believe unquestionably that Allah is the Islamic god. It is deemed that Allah is the all powerful creator. He is transmundane and not part of his creation. Extraordinarily, the Quran uncovers 99 disparate names for god (*Asma al-Husna*) and the following are purported to be the most prudent and popular; the creator, the fashioner, the life-giver, the provider, the opener, the bestowed, the prevailed, the reckoner and the recorder. The commonality and convenience of the names has made them attractive to those who are Muslim in consonance with the Quran but also with those who are counterfeit or Muslims by chance. According to Hassan Rouhani, who chastised his Iranian leaders, there is a substantial number of pretenders who act as a Muslim publicly (Out of fear of losing their head) but contradict their "righteous" actions privately.

The distinct difference between the god Allah, who is revealed only through his messengers and is therefore personally obscure and remote; and the Biblical God, is that He can be known personally through His Son, His Spirit and of course, His Scriptures. The question of god is far from being new. In the pre-Islamic era and even prior to that in early Arabic times, the question of god was prevalent. Some faiths, such as the Roman Catholic, chose to major on the similarities between the two; Allah and God. On the other hand, antipodal Christians quite naturally turn to what is different and not what is the same. Another prominent point is that if one reads the

Quran, it soon becomes glaringly obvious that any personal and intimate relationship with Allah is an inconsequential thought. The pages plainly state that Allah knows his people but not once does it directly say his people know him. This is in stark contrast to another monotheistic religion called Christianity. Here, we find no fewer than 83 relevant verses that express a mutual relationship that is planted in love and grown in grace. The prophet Jeremiah provides a prime example; Thus says the Lord: "Let not the wise man boast in his wisdom, let not the mighty man boast in his might, let not the rich man boast in his riches, but let him who boasts boast in this, that he understands and knows Me, that I am the Lord who practices steadfast love, justice, and righteousness in the earth. For in these things I delight, declares the Lord." To be able to boast in God requires as a pre-requisite, that we must first "know" Him. It is inconceivable that a person would boast about someone they have never met.

When it comes to the concept of God, we learn that the Allah of Islam predestines the lives of mankind with a propensity for good and evil. Submission to "Allah's Will" means that mankind has no responsibility of its own. What is good and evil cannot be determined rationally, but only by the exhortations of the Quran and Muhammad. For instance, the difference between the god of the Quran and the God of the Bible is as far from the east as it is from the west. The stark undeniable difference between these two is profound. Allah demands that his followers know the "holy book" which is the antithesis of the Biblical Book, where God commands his followers to first know Him, as the author and finisher! Knowing a book is one thing but knowing the writer is everything. The orthodox Islamic jurisprudence affirms and repeats that god is Allah (Arabic for the god) and Allah produced the Quran (holy book) for Muhammad (most praised) to instruct Muslims (followers) in the religion of Islam (submission). This is something of an over-simplification and it is purposely intended to be so as up to seventy five percent of adherents to this repugnant "religion" say they do not understand what is being mouthed in the Mosque. The New Statesman adopts a similar stance by enunciating that between 2000-2010 over 100,000 of the U.K. population extemporaneously converted to Islam. Regrettably, Islamism is one of those apocryphal religious systems that people become easily entangled in. Mormonism is a comparable cult.

Both these prickly systems function like barbed wire; snaring or snagging the unsuspecting person. This is reinforced by the dramatic fall-out from the earlier 100,000 "conversions" being almost half that number.

We believe it would be sententious at this point to draw attention to this generic word "religion." The primary issue when discussing this term is that it tends to generate more heat than light. We also often discover that this subject is embraced too casually and even carelessly. Therefore, it is imperative that we apply a degree of sensitively and sensibility. Take Islam for instance; how frequently it is that we hear and read it propounded as, "The Religion of Peace." Both Muslims and others are known to favour these four words to exemplify Islam. Even, the main sects of Islam, Sunni and Shia, who never seem to see eye to eye; find it convenient to use the same phrase. At this juncture in the proceedings we find ourselves lodged between the cleft of a rock and a hard place; Islam being the hard place and its religion the cleft of a rock. There are many who firmly believe that Islam is not a religion but those who will actually vocalise that fact are few and far between. The accomplished author, Rebecca Bynum, has stuck her neck out by naming one of her books, "Allah is Dead." She then has the fortitude to write, "Islam is not a religion." Those two comments alone, are sufficient to invoke the wrath of every merciless Muslim in the world.

What makes such statements so disquieting is that they are perfectly true. The Quran mentions man's heart (depending on scholar and translation) in different forms, a total of 241 times. Yet, the heart of Allah is conspicuous by its absence and leaves the reader grasping the truth that Allah is heartless and lifeless. The two words Islam and religion are uncomfortably incompatible. Islam's source flows from these three main streams, Quran, Hadith and Sira. We ascertain from Robert Spencer, "It is widely acknowledged that the Quran is more of a political treaty than it is a spiritual strategy." The think tank Pew Research maintains, "The majority view of the American populace is that Sharia should not be promoted but instead it should be banished." Unfortunately, two British prime ministers, Cameron and May, have ignored the alarm bells and have given a green light to "sharia laws" being implemented. For the Muslim it was just the thin end of the wedge. Within a decade those "few laws" would soon number over a hundred Sharia Law Courts littering the landscape. Cunningly, Islam has hoodwinked the politicians in to believeing that the laws are merely domestic guidelines and not the draconian measures they have proven to be. The short sighted-ness of May and the government regarding Sharia Law, has meant we are one step coser to national suicide.

Across the water in Europe, we find that the fallout from Sharia is having a disasterous impact. Austria is drowning in Islam and Sharia Laws are being detonated like land mines. The nations future is unpredictable and its status as a country is in the democratic balance. Joshua (not his real name) lives in Vienna with his family. They decided to make a contribution to the migrant mayhem so they made friends with a Muslim migrant man. After a short while he started to get into bed with their 10 year old son. This went on for a week or so and before the 10 year old boy mustered up enough courage to tell his parents; he had been sodomised 63 times. This is typical and the general practice, particularly in Afghanistan. When questioned, endless excuses dribbled out of the Muslim's mouth. If this were confined just to Austria we would still be as horrified but regrettably it has smeared and stained much of the European landscape. Sweden has surrendered and Germany have capitulated. They have so many sexual crimes that they have lost count. In the U.K. it is true to say that such lascivious behaviour is more likely to be thrown out of court rather than the culprits thrown into prison. Since the Prime Minister of the U.K. is comprehensively compromised; her cabinet and country are now unavoidably implicated. If you believe the press and we do not, up to 100,000 sexual offences were carried out by Muslim's in Britain in just over decade (Geller Report). Both the government and the public are now in cognitive denial. Norman Khan's comment here is very accommodating; "The British government and gullible public habitually state, not all Muslim's are terrorist's." This is the knee jerk reaction after every terrorist act. But what is also pertinent is the other side of the coin – while all Muslim's may not be terrorist's we can safely say that all terrorist's are Muslim.

It was not until the 1990's that we began in Britain to regularly and repeatedly hear about dispicable Islamic crimes such rape, acid attacks, suicide bombers, sharia law, knife attacks, decapitating infidel's, child brides, immolation, vehicle ramming, missing persons and countless other acts of atrocity. How quickly the international scene varies and how often the political stage changes. People like Obama and his right hand man, Biden, are bellowing peace, peace when there is no peace. In contrast to those two charlatans, Dr. Daniel Pipes admits; "This is no longer simply a taste of things to come." Pipes perception is that it has already arrived – it is in our face right now, yet the west is lamentably in a deep coma. It is unconscious and without any sense that the enemy is crouching at the door. Pipe (Middle East Forum) prompts us to take a look at what is on the American doorstep..... mass Muslim migration, multiple mosque building, proselytising in prisons, Islamic ghetto's, sharia patrols, no-go zones, forced marriages and so-called honour killings which are all common occurrences. The "honour" killings are perhaps the single most underrated and unreported felony. A typical text book honour killing happened in 2009 (MacleansNews). The perpetrator of the four murders was an Afghan called Mohammed Shafia. He was regarded as a pious and punctilious man. The victims? His own three beautiful teenage daughters and lovely wife. But what exactly was his grievance? What on earth did they do to warrant being killed? The four females were guilty of simply chatting to some passing boys. Under Sharia this is a capital offence and since Muslim's have a vocabulary devoid of mercy these women were doomed. The last words of the murderer, Mohammed, after he wiped the blade clean of blood, "I would do it again a hundred times." This is unadulterated ugly Islam. Once again we are faced with a vile illustration of the devilish deeds of "The Bloody Religion of Peace."

Allah and Islam is more unique than we have already intimated. The god Allah, and many believe that he never existed except in the mind of deluded Arabs; is the only god that retains his followers with fear and force. In order to produce proselytes, Dr. Wood draws a distinction; "Allah employs the blade of the sword to gain converts but antithetically God has the Sword of the Spirit which is the Word of God." How wretched that Muslim's live by fear rather than by faith. We read in the Quran (Quran 9:5) Muslim's are to slay Christian's but the Bible impalpably commands Christian's to love their enemies. The Bible is explicit and emphatic, there are no innuendo's in any of the 66 books but there are warnings; "Every spirit which does not acknowledge that Jesus has come in the flesh... is the spirit of the Antichrist..." Again, David Wood contributes; "The conclusion is circumscribed; the spirit in Islam is the spirit of the Antichrist." It is highly significant that Muhammad, who spent years amongst Jews and Christian's; still denied Christ. Judas and Muhammad are anomalously placed in history and both are memorable for identical reasons. Judas spent three long years with Jesus but in the end he still denied Him. The Lord says, "...If you deny me... I will deny you..." We have every reason to believe the Apostle, Mark; both these men have gone where the fire is never quenched and the worm never dies and it is solely because they denied Jesus was the Christ.

One has to search long and hard to find something remotely positive about Islam's Allah. Unfortunately the longer and deeper you delve into Islam, the more obnoxious and odious it becomes. Divine and Allah are mismatched terms that do not deserve to be in the same sentence. It is argued convincingly, by David Letterman, "Islam's Allah was not the God of whom the pre-Islamic Arabs worshipped as their god, but was the alter-ego of manic Muhammad." There is every reason to believe that all the words of the Quran are Muhammad's own, which he surreptitiously put on the tongue of his fictitious friend Allah (AKA Muhammad). We can confidently confirm that when the evidence is placed on the scales, Allah will be found wanting. The evil in the supposedly "holy book" percolates from from cover to cover. If we place the Penthouse, Playboy and Quran side by side, which one would we consider to be the most abhorrent? It has to be the Quran because it is there that Allah fosters hatred, encourages violence and incites murder. He pronounces death to the kafir or infidel.

In the Islamic "library" of literature the first 100 books all have something peculiarly generic. Apart from Allah's authority, they are all inundated with extended episodes of truculence. In spite of reading and knowing this, the vast majority of the public believe that Allah and "The Religion of Peace" are simply some sort of harmless platitude. This is the concerted national cry after every Muslim terrorist attack by Allah: "It is nothing to do with Islam." George Bush said after 9/11, Tony Blair said after 7/7, Tony Abbot said after 11/15 and David Cameron said after the soldier Lee

Rigby was decapitated by two cowardly Muslims, "This is nothing to do with Islam." It will not come as any surprise to learn Francis Hollande said exactly the same thing after the massacre of journalists and Jews, "This is nothing to do with Islam." Each leader told a bare faced lie and showed no shame. Each one of the above knew when they made those cowhearted denials of Islam that they were guilty of prevaricating.

Every one of these leaders and more, are not just horribly wrong but are downright dishonest. They know they are lying, so why do so many "upright" men tell lies? There are two reasons, or, perhaps excuses, for their dishonesty. They would say it's a "noble lie" to spare the public from the fear that terrorism fosters. Another reason is that it minimises misunderstanding. If the public remain ignorant they will not know how serious the threat is and being oblivious will only promote a false sense of security. Of course, one could devote a whole book just to the evil of Allah and there would be no shortage of material. Perhaps, the most infamous teaching to fall from Allah's "mouth" is that which has dropped on to the pages of his "holy book."

> "Then, when the sacred months have passed, slay the idolater wherever ye find them, and take them (captive), and besiege them, and prepare for them each ambush. But if they repent and establish worship and pay the poor-due, then leave their way free. Lo! Allah is Forgiving, Merciful." It is a most murderous passage that is wholly consistent with a monstrous god (Quran 9:5).

Commenting on the magnitude of such a vitriolic verse, Ali Al-bin Ali explicates: "This hideous verse tells and teaches Muslim's to commit mass-murder (Allah is Merciful!). The kaffirs must either convert to Islam, who would keep up prayer and pay the poor-rate (*zakat*), or be mercilessly murdered. A command for unconditional slaying of humans, God's own creations, by other humans – when presented as a sacred teaching of the almighty Creator – becomes a most noxious teaching. Needless to say, such instructions never originated with God in heaven." Wickedness of such proportion can only be contained in one place; it must be held and housed in hell.

The most popular angle from which many people pursue their understanding of Allah is by starting with his name. What follows is differences and disagreements over his name *Allah* (the god or the moon god). Since this issue of his secondary names has already been dealt with in general, we will examine Allah, not by his name but rather by his nature. Some people have had the most appealing names but the most appalling natures. One can argue convincingly that the person's nature is far more determining than the name. When we read the Bible (James 1:13) we discern that God cannot be tempted by evil and neither does he tempt any one with evil, "For thou are not a God that hath pleasure in wickedness" (Psalm 5:4). Yet, when we read the Quran we discover that Allah is the author of evil (Surah 4:142; 3:54; 8:30; 10:21). The term "scheme" employed in the above verses is the Arabic word *makara* which denotes one who is a deceiver, conniver and schemer. Allah is thus seen as superior when it comes to deceiving, conniving and scheming. We must be careful here not to fall in to the pit called prejudice. This view or opinion exceeds the Christian perimeters and also encompasses the perceptions of Islamic theologians. It is highly significant that a leading Islamic academic, Dr. Mahmoud M. Ayoub renders the same word "makara" as "plotting or scheming". What is more crucial is that he expressly attributes this wicked word to god or Allah. In his book, "The Quran and its Interpreters," he is found resoundly applying the word "evil" in the context of the Islamic deity. The scholar Shamoun, who is from the same camp as Ayoub, is not simply to attribute the name makara to Allah but exposits the word as a definitive description of Allah's very nature.

Just when the Muslim thought things could not get worse, they do. Our analysis shows that Allah is not alone. Muhammad is apparently painted with the same bloody brush and cannot be trusted. The Muslim contention is that it is only non-believers who are on the receiving end of deception. This assertion is not water tight as it is riddled with holes. Muslims busy themselves trying to plug the holes but the Quranic scriptures are as plain as day. Allah did not only deceive Muhammad over the Battle of Badr but he also bamboozled the unbelievers (Surah 8:43-44). There is one matter which is too important to bypass. Of all Allah's dastardly deeds, his greatest lie surrounded the crucifixion of Christ. According to the Quran

Jesus was not crucified but Allah fabricated a phoney version to delude the masses. Not content to be a deceiver, the Islamic deity, Allah, quotes in the Quran that he actually raises wicked individuals to dole out deception (Surah 6:123). He then further instructs people to perpetrate evil so that he has a "legitimate" reason to destroy them (Surah 17:16).

When the Quran is opened wide we fall over another word that denotes that Allah is a liar with guile or *kayd:* "And those who cry lies to Our signs we will draw them on little by little when they know not; and I respite them – assuredly my guile (*kaydee*) is sure" (Surah 7:182-183). In the lexicons we see revealed the following definitions in this same respect: "Kaf-Ya-Dal – to perform an artful device, desire, contrive/plot/devise such a thing...to deceive/beguile/circumvent"(Surah 68:45).

The Quran is replete with examples that exemplify the negative nature of this term, e.g. those who use *kayd* are deliberately manufacturing something that is essentially execrable which results in their judgement and disaster for employing such wicked schemes (Surah's 7:195, 12.5). In one text Allah is portrayed as stooping down to the same level as the deceivers and liars by acting just like them in his use of guile: "They are devising guile and I am (Allah) devising greater guile" (Surah 86:15-16).

If you thought that there could not possibly be anything else, you would be wrong. There is more to the story. When we turn over a page in the Quran we find yet another word describing the Muslim god Allah, that word being *khida/khuda/khada:* "Verily, the hypocrites seek to deceive Allah, but it is he who deceives them." Once again we find the same lexical root word: "Kh-Dal-Ayn – to hide/conceal, or deceive/outwit, refrain or refuse, to deviate from the right course. Do not make the mistake of many by applying this to Allah's subjects for each word applies explicitly to Allah. The exegete, Samuel Shamoun, supplies the following to support this view: "Lest there be any confusion concerning the fact that this word means that Allah is a deceiver. (Surah 2:9) Is there any doubt that the unbelievers were using deception as they tried to deceive Muhammad and his companions? Just as there is no doubt that Allah also uses deception in duly deceiving them."

We come to a controversial part or a potentially volatile passage. Satan accused Allah of misleading or deceiving him. He said: "Now, because thou hast sent me astray *(aghwaytanee)*, verily I shall lurk in ambush for them on Thy Right Path" (Surah 7:16). Satan said, "O my Lord! Because you misled me *(aghwaytanee)*, I shall indeed adorn the path of error for them (mankind) on the earth, and I shall mislead *(walaoghwiyannahum)* them all" (Surah 15:39). What makes this last reference so significant is that Satan promises to do to mankind what Allah did to him, namely, pervert/deceive/mislead people from the path! Lest a Muslim say that these are the lies of Satan, that the enemy was merely slandering Allah, here is a text where the Quran acknowledges that the Devil was right since Allah does pervert/deceive and mislead people away from the way. "And my sincere counsel will not profit you, if I desire to counsel you sincerely, if god desires to pervert you *(yughwiyakum)*; he is your Lord, and unto Him you shall be returned (Surah 11:34). Who knows this? Who ever reads this? Ambivalence means the number is few and far between."

The remarks above should not only open our eyes but also our mouths. The analysis has shown that Muhammad's "deity" is a deceiver who cannot be trusted since he is a habitual liar. A Muslim may contend that Allah only deceives unbelievers who deserve it. The problem with this assertion is that the Muslim scripture tells and teaches that Allah does not merely deceive unbelievers but also his followers. For example, Allah deceived Muhammad into thinking that the fighting men at Badr were fewer in number than they actually were. "When Allah showed them to you in your dream as few; and if He had shown them to you as many you would certainly have become weak-hearted and you would have disputed about the matter, but Allah saved (you); surely he is is the Knower of what is in the breasts. And when he showed them to you, when you met, as a few in your eyes and He made you appear to be a little in their eyes, in order that Allah might bring about a certain matter which was to be done, and to Allah are all affairs returned" (Surah 8:43-44).

These words do nothing but condemn Allah. This derisory narrative is not found in many books but it is found in The Muslim Book. We have not resorted to making a partisan personal attack but have sought only to submit an objective observation taken from Islamic material including the "Holy Quran." From our extrapolations we discern that Allah lies and deceives both believers and unbelievers without discrimination or conscience. He is clearly cerebrally cauterized since His conscience shows none of the vital signs of life. When the God of the Bible informed the prophet Jeremiah (17:9), "The heart is deceitful and above all things desperately wicked," we have every reason to suppose that in making this affirmation God included Allah's defiled heart. In contrast to him we hear the God of Yahweh say on at least ten occasions; "God is not a man, that He should lie, nor a son of man, that he should change His mind" (numbers 23:19). If we were a private detective, the evidence of the Quran's description of Allah would lead us to the one whom the Lord identified as the "father of lies." The same sentiment is written in John's (8:44) gospel where we read "You (a liar) belong to your father, the devil, and you want to carry out your father's desire. He was a murderer from the beginning, not holding on to the truth, for there is no truth in him." When a person lies he is consciously guilty of speaking the devil's native language, for he is a liar and even the father of lies. A jury would have no difficlty in reaching a verdict for the judge and the adjudication would ultimately be unanimous – Allah, the accused, is guilty (lying) as charged.

In light of the foregoing it seems rather hard to deny that the spirit who spoke to Muhammad, the entity who is revealed in the Muslim Scripture, is none other than Satan, who the Bible states is the enemy of our souls. This is the one who masquerades as God in order to deceive people and draw them away from the truth of the Gospel of the Lord Jesus Christ. Furthermore, the description of Allah emphatically articulated by Christ, is who the Christian Apologist Jay Smith accredits as the evil angelic being who fell from heaven. There is a disparity amongst eschatologists concerning the identity of Antichrist. Scholars such as Slick is convinced that Allah explicitly fits the profile of Satan. Prophetic proponents like Irvin Baxter are more reticent and would refer to Allah and Islam as having the spirit of Antichrist; "...every spirit that does not acknowledge Jesus is not from God. This is the spirit of the Antichrist, which you have heard coming and even now is already in the world." (1 John 4:3). Islamic doctrine denounces the deity of Christ and relegates Him to merely a prophet. The delusion by Allah, by his own confession, denies that Jesus is the Christ and in doing so signs his fate and orders his demise.

Since you will not read this in the press (fake), it is imperative to afford it the time it deserves now. Through the highly effective indoctrination, the Islamist's have come to believe the lie of all lies. Islam's apparition is that they have swallowed, hook, line and sinker that Allah is "the god." This means that the Muslim will stick to the will of Allah like a limpet to a rock. The upshot is that a Muslim will blindly say what Allah says and do what Allah does. Although the dominant theme of the delusion is quasi spiritual, the promised rewards of the afterlife are exclusively carnal. Everything that the Jihadist fails to do in this life will be purified and proffered in the next life. Allah is the author of an instruction manual called Islam, which details "human" behaviour. Amil Amani, writes, "the mullahs manipulate the brain of the Jihadi so that his normal human instinct is violated. The brain is disabled to such an extent that the Muslim is used as you would a tool. When they have completely succumbed under the weight of blind subjugation, Muslim's are left preferring death to life. The greatest threat to civilisation is not climate change, nor politics, or economics. Civilisation is currently in the balance and the only hope it has is defeating and disarming the global threat of Islamisation, that is being engineered through the vehicle of Islamofascism.

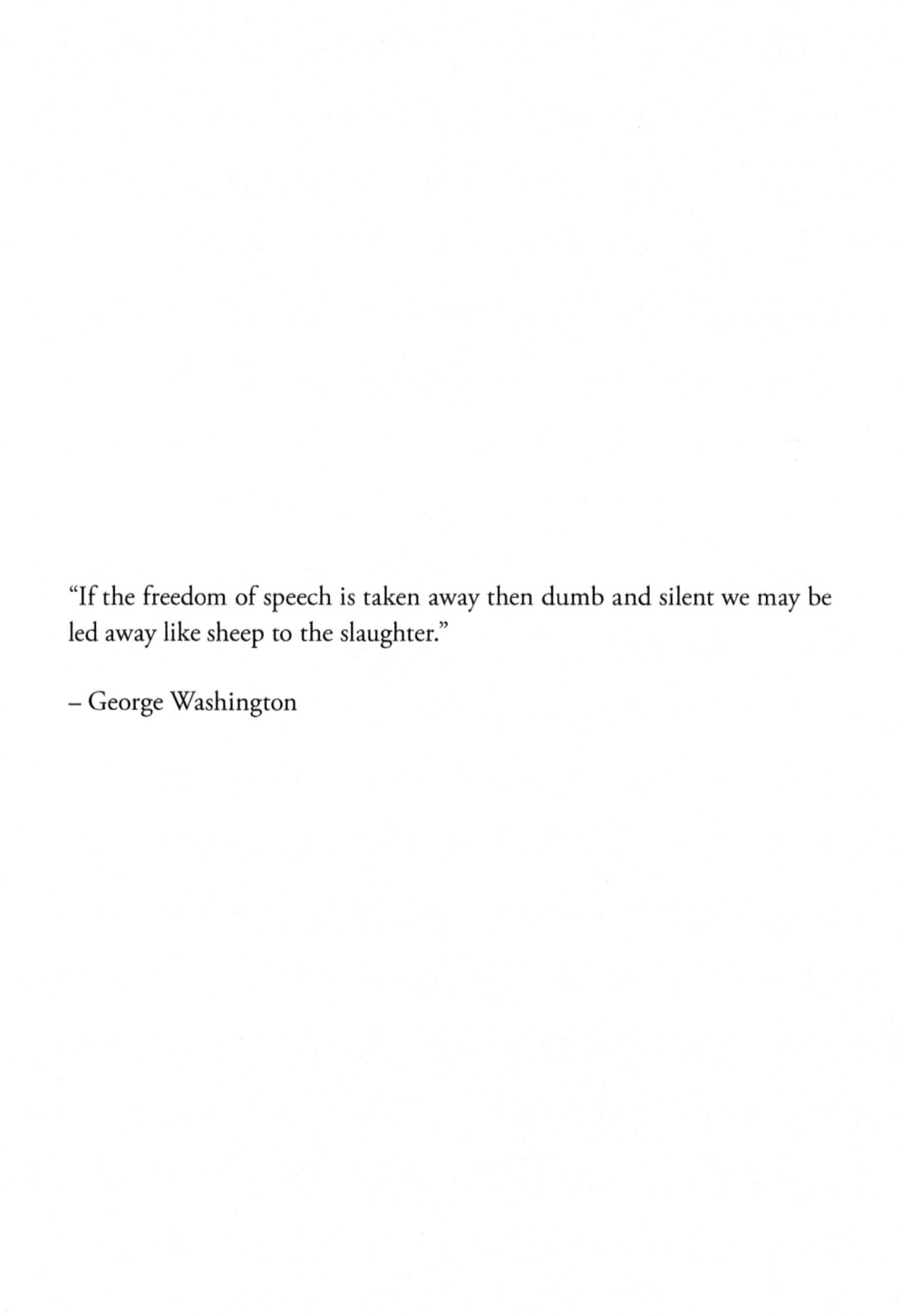

"If the freedom of speech is taken away then dumb and silent we may be led away like sheep to the slaughter."

– George Washington

Chapter Two

Muhammad

"The conscience is the most dangerous thing you possess. If you wake it up and disobey it, it may destroy you."

- J. P. Stanley.

The man Muhammad (570-632) was born in Mecca, Saudi Arabia, after his father, Abdullah ibn Abdul-Muttalib; met his "maker." At the age of six his mother, Amina bint Wahb also suddenly died, leaving him in the care of relatives. During his formative years Muhammad spent an inordinate amount of time travelling on Christian camel trains as they traversed the barren Arabian desert. There is much evidence to show he interacted with Christians and was influenced by prominent believers such as Waraqa ibn Nawfal. We are told by pundit Ismail Acar that Muhammad had a lengthy encounter with a tribe called the Najran Christians. Not surprisingly, we soon discover a remote shadow of similarity between the Quranic passages and the Biblical texts, which is far from being coincidental. Historical author, Gerald Hawting, reveals that there are fifty Quranic references to Biblical characters and a certain congruence with some stories. It was during this period that Muhammad fashioned an understanding of Christianity which would be instrumental in his construction of the Quran. The self-appointed prophet went on to spend his life divided between driving camels and killing people. Muhammad's own death in Medina was as ignominious as his life, being poisoned by one of an increasing legion of disaffected followers. Cracks were beginning to appear in the make-up of the prophet and what people saw and heard, enamoured them less.

What they will not tell you in the mosque is that Muhammad, allegedly the last prophet of god, was a man with a variety of titles – some you would approve of and some you would not. Two titles that Muslim's endeavour to bury at all cost; are occasionally resurrected, albeit much to the disapproval of Islam. The first concerns his lifestyle and his preoccupation with hedonism. Muhammad lived a life of opulence, engaging in excesses which did much for his belly but nothing for his heart. His over-indulgence was justified by so-called revelations from a capricious god, which he used to quantify and qualify his bizarre behaviour. As a cult leader he was dogmatic and demanded utter obedience from his followers. His self-seeking selfishness stretched to him instructing his men to keep his commandments if they were to please Allah (Quran 4:80, 59:7). He was doing then exactly what the Pope does now and act as a go-between, or an advocate between god and man. In later years Muhammad incorrigibly exploited his influence to satisfy his hedonistic appetite. This included personal goals, sexual desires, wealth and power. Allah's authority for him to pursue these earthly ambitions is immortalised in the Quran (Sura's 33 and 66). This is the same man who stated at the outset of his career as a prophet, "I asked for no reward from others." It was not long before he reneged on that promise and began to demand between 30%-40% of all booty taken from conquered tribes. According to his biographers he became grossly overweight, even fat, from his self indulgences and ill-gotten gains. In the next decade it was the same trend of excesses. Muhammad married 13 women and possessed a countless number of sex slaves. If he wanted another wife or woman he would simply exercise his authority and take what he wanted, including children. The prophet was able to justify his lust and inevitable consummation with an appeal to Allah's revealed will for his sex life. This was preserved in the Quran forever, to be faithfully memorised by future generations for whom it has no possible relevance whatsoever.

A feature of Muhammad's life is one that no-one inside Islam would want to discuss. It is refuted repeatedly and denied vehemently. One of the reasons that this particular flaw is kept under wraps by Muslims is the sense of shame that is attached to it. In the Quran (Sura 33:21) Muhammad is trumpeted as the perfect pattern for Muslims to follow. Yet, the trusted early sources turn that suggestion upside down. These are the words of Muhammad according to philosopher Iban Shag;

> "I awoke from my sleep, and it was as though these words were written on my heart. None of god's creatures was more hateful to me than a poet or possessed: I could not even look at them. I thought, Woe is me poet or possessed—never shall Squashy say this of me! I will go to the top of the mountain and throw myself down that I may kill myself and gain rest. So I went forth to do so and then when I was midway on the mountain, I heard a voice from heaven saying, "O Muhammad! Thou art the apostle of God and I am Gabriel."

We suggest again that a suicidal prone prophet is not the perfect pattern for any one to follow, let alone Muslim's. A leader who is pre-occupied with throwing himself off the mountain top is not some one who should be followed. His dicing with death was not an isolated occurrence. Sahih al-Bukhari (6982), a highly esteemed scholar, writes extensively on this dark and secret episode in the prophet's life, where he is said to have had multiple thoughts and attempts of suicide. The Islamic historians with integrity, all agree on the method of suicide but when it comes to the motivation there is considerable disparity. If we look over our shoulder to the earliest biographical record on the life of Muhammad, the prophet of Islam attempted to kill himself then. Now comes the missing motivation or reason. Muhammad believed he was possessed by an evil spirit and we confidently confirm that there are multitudes who who share that belief. The same conclusion is reached by ibn Ishaq, Al-Tabari and Tarikh al-Rusl. Muhammad's savage behaviour toward those he met and killed, would make it difficult to argue that he belonged to the human race. Spending one's life courting suicide and being consumed by an "evil" spirit would most certainly disqualify him from any office let alone as a prophet of god.

The life and death of Muhammad is aptly encapsulated in the memorable Bible verse; "...For all who draw the sword will die by the sword" (Matthew 26:52). It is not a synchronism that Muhammad, the mass-murderer, is a fulfilment of this incisive excerpt of Scripture. Muhammad will be remembered for a medley of things but one of the most reported and repeated is as "prophet." Over the centuries many people have claimed to be an apostle. The problem with this is that the messages are invariably all said to be of god but they inevitably contradict one another. The stumbling block here is that just because someone claims to be a prophet is no guarantee that he is. There are several ways to overcome this obstacle. Firstly, the person may be getting the "revelation" from his own imagination. He might be utterly sincere but it is within the realms of possibility; to be sincerely wrong. Secondly, it is likely for the person to obtain their revelations from demonic sources. If that is the case then it will mean a double deception for both prophet and hearer. Thirdly, the revelation may actually come from "god," in which case everyone should summarily obey what the true god declares.

The world in which we live is short of many commodities but false prophets is not one of them. What we find today is that there is not a shortage but a surplus of false prophets stretching from America to Africa and Asia. In this respect, Muslim's are not reluctant to question Christ's credibility as a prophet but their own prophet is blindly accepted, exalted and exaggerated out of recognition. This leaves the public pondering whether Muhammad is in fact, a false prophet? Christ's warning is incisive, "Beware of false prophets who come to you in sheep clothing but inwardly are ravenous wolves." These words sound like an alarm bell and should wake all those who have been unwittingly seduced in to a deep sleep.

It is worth noting at this juncture that when people discuss Christ they feel free to scorn, scandalise, deride, blaspheme, vilify and trample Him under their feet, and they do it without shame or hesitation. However, if the table is turned and Muhammad is scrutinised and criticised, we can be sure that the subsequent Muslim fall-out would be highly radio-active. In terms of Muhammad there is much that can be said. To all intensive purposes we could easily conceive that his prophet-hood was more sensual than spiritual. It is apparent that Islam's emphasis was not on "being" but "doing." Muhammad the prophet dictated that Muslims had to pray five times – praying facing Mecca; they must take an annual pilgrimage (*hajj*) to Mecca, where they circled the oblique Kabah and kissed the opprobrious black stone that apparently fell or flew from "paradise."

The consistently burning question being whispered is whether Muhammad was the real deal or not. This question is one that few people would dare to ask privately let alone voice publicly. The question is an impolitic one in these politically correct turbulent times. It is significant that virtually all of the terrorism in the world (91%) and the number of Jihad's at large (25%) all emanate from the spurious so-called "religion of peace" that Muhammad founded (Islamic Evil Report). With this fact in view it begs the question is Muhammad of the Quran authentic or fraudulent? It is an undeniable fact, established by C.A.R.M. (Christian Apologetics) that there is no shortage of false prophets peppering the world; in fact, we have more now than at any time in history. If it proves true that Muhammad is as false as the million copies of the Mona Lisa hanging in French homes, then it must mean Islam is also a fake. What is mystifying is the number of people who are prepared to accept Muhammadan's at face value, without even so much as a question. Why are leaders of religious bodies and European heads of state so eager to seek solidarity with Muhammadan's and the inconsonantly named "religion of peace?" The Pope and Cardinal's are bedevilled to such an extent they are kissing the feet of terrorist's in the Vatican. The same mass-murderers who threatened the Pope's head would be on a plate just as John the Baptist was. The Church of England Bishop's have been beguiled! They are permitting clergy to read the Quran instead of the Bible in their church and are welcoming Muslim Cleric's to "preach" to congregations and all with the Archbishop's blessing. Merkel has surrendered and will metaphorically, sleep with any imam in any Mosque. She has been harshly labelled by the extreme German left, as a "political slut." Then there's anaemic Stefan Lofven the compromised leader of Sweden who has capitulated. His police are paralysed. Sexual crimes in Sweden are greater than all the Scandinavian countries combined. Rape is up 97% and 97% of the culprits are migrants. Swedish women are going to inordinate lengths to become less attractive. They are colouring their hair any colour but blonde and dressing down whenever they venture out.

Strikingly, it was in Sweden that one of the more grotesque Islamic crimes was committed. A young 14 year old Muslim girl was violently gang raped by some Muslim migrant men and critically traumatised. When her older brother discovered this he set about making things right. No, he did not pursue the men and seek retribution. That would be the more civilised solution. However, since he was uncivilised, he vented his vicious fury on his sister. She had brought shame on the family and deserved to be punished according to sinister Sharia Islamic law said she should pay the ultimate price and so he coldly killed her – he murdered his own young sister for being raped. Geller is absolutely right when she calls Islam "savages." On the same day in a sunny suburb of Stockholm, a woman was making her way home when she was approached by 20 Muslim migrants. They made a circle around her and one by one the twenty callously raped and sodomised her. When they had finished they left her in the gutter half dead. This poor woman, only partially clothed, crawled to find the nearest police while all her cowardly neighbours hid behind their calico curtains. Before long she found what she thought was help but when the police saw her they backed off. Their response was, "We cannot touch you as you are covered in semen which is probably has different diseases." Many of the migrants have rabies from bestiality and sexual diseases from multiple rapes.

Living in Europe is beginning to resemble fish living in a bowl. Governments are not proactively turning stones over in search of terrorists. What is happening is that nations simply bide their time until the next attack comes. Heads of government apparently have their fingers in their ears hoping the next explosion is not too loud. We have multiple crimes occurring by the day but European countries behave like an addict who is in deep denial. The reaction to each crime is first to diminish it and then second to dismiss it. An Eritrean teenager begs at the German border to be given a new life. He says he's been traumatised by the war at home. Europe swings open the gate and in walks our "refugee." His idea of settling in to the country and becoming a decent citizen takes less than a week. A problem materialised with a fellow asylum seeker owing him almost $50. Rather than discuss it, the 18 year old Eritrean has an alternative means of resolving the matter. He removes two knives from the sheaths and his first act is to cut off the eyelids of the teen who owed him money. The next brutality is to stab him in both eyes so the points of the knives are sticking in his eyeballs. Lastly, he brutally bites off his ears and chews them so they cannot be sewn back on. His lawyer is making a case around diminished responsibility and cultural diversity. Crimes of this nature, savage crimes, are a regular occurrence. This not an isolated or rare example. Each hour a criminal offence is perpetrated in a European country and 98% of the criminals are ostensibly migrants or refugees.

One of the hinges on which the Prophet's doctrine swings is if Muhammad is true or whether Jesus is true. Since they contradict each other it is the contrast between the two prophets, Jesus and Muhammad. The two accounts are remarkably different so it impossible for both to be true. In the New Testament Jesus is imperious that He is the Son of God but the Quran is insistent that He is not. Since Muhammad is the main subject here and not Jesus, let us consider the underlying Quranic portions that state the opposite to Jesus:

- God is but one god. God forbid that he should have a son (4:173).
- The Messiah, the Son of Mary, was no more than an apostle (5:75).
- Christians call Christ the the son of Allah...Allah's curse be on them: how they have departed from the truth! (9:30).
- They do blaspheme who say: Allah is one of the three in a Trinity (5:73).
- A book titled "The Same God" by Ralph Sidway proves without a shadow of doubt the complete opposite of the book's title.

If we glance at the handful of examples above it is immediately evident; so obvious, that "The Man in the Moon" can see there is no resemblance whatsoever, between Jesus and Muhammad. When we take the book the "Same God Question" and distil it down to its finest particle, we are left with the conclusion that revelation proves what has been affirmed; Allah and Muhammad and God and Jesus, are poles apart – it is a divine dissonance. We can conclude that the author of the Quran not only refutes but rapaciously rejects the concept of the Trinity. Furthermore, he makes the declaration that a "grievous penalty will fall" on those who persist in saying that "Allah is one of three" (Sura 5:73). The hostility of puss pouring from Allah's mouth towards Christ's Christianity, says linguist Sidway; is surely tantamount to a "Theological Jihad."

There is a question that is often asked but seldom answered. Why, why did Muhammad bother to include Jesus in the Quran? Writer William Kilpatrick proves positive when he articulates: "Muhammad's purpose in introducing Jesus to the Quran is twofold. Firstly, Muhammad wanted to discredit the Christian claim that Jesus is divine. Secondly, in doing this Muhammad could then exalt his own claim to premier prophet. If Christ is who Christians say He is, then there would be absolutely no need for another prophet. This revelation would leave Muhammad high and dry and any prospects of a career in prophecy dismissed. In the Old Testament the people were dissatisfied with the God they were given, so they decided to make their own. On one occasion they made an image of a golden calf to foolishly worship. Instead of man being created in the image of God the rebellious people made a god created in the image of man. Allah is the antithesis of this and has the affront to repeatedly assimilate the wisdom of man is foolishness to God"

Many centuries later Muhammad fell in to the same pit and did the same thing with Jesus. He moronically made Him in to the image of man – of himself. Whatever Muhammad's motivation might be, the irreducible truth is that the Jesus of the Bible and the Jesus of the Qur'an are irreconcilable. Since both are decidedly different how can both revelations be from the same God? If Jesus Christ is God, then Muhammad was merely masquerading as the last prophet. Going around stating such things about Muhammad to people, will inevitably mean a reduced life expectancy. One of facts peculiar to Muslims is that they are notoriously bad at is discussing, dialogue and debating. Needless to say the fall out from any controversial exchange will predictably come crashing down on the dreaded dhimmi's head.

I suppose we could conjure up our own Muhammad; we might go as far as to make Muhammad in our own image. We could even go further and say, well he was not all bad – he did have some good points, even though I cannot find them. It is true, we cannot deny that Muhammad did make one or two intelligent decisions but on this vital point of Christ's divinity, the New Testament leaves no room for doubt. The Gospel's are emphatic on this matter, "He who is not with Me is against Me" (Luke 11: 23. Jesus does not leave any room for a soft seat on the fence. The Bible makes it perfectly plain, "In Him we live and move and have our being" (Acts 17:28). Acceptance of Christ's divinity is like possessing the skeleton key that opens all the doors. Much is made of Muhammad the "prophet." One of the most asked questions about this man is whether he was a false or true prophet? Webster's original 1828 dictionary defines a prophet as: "One that foretells future events." In Scripture the prophet was the one who was directly inspired to reveal God's word and His will. When it came to the crunch between the prophet hood's of Christ and Muhammad, we find there is no contest. Muhammad's prophetic performance is perplexingly pitiful. In contrast, Christ's, prophecies have thus far been 100% correct. The last prophecy He made occurred when He was on the cross and where He told his hearers what conditions would be like prior to his second coming. This was of course not his final prophecy as unfulfilled prophetic passages are yet to be executed. In the Old Testament, over 300 prophecies are directly attributed to Christ and all were realised.

One of the authenticating proofs for the inspiration of the Bible is the claims of Jesus Christ as the Son of God and the Saviour of the World. The discussion of Biblical prophecy is an extremely extensive subject. We have the Old and the New testaments and of course we have the Prophecy before and after Christ. Theologian Wayne Jackson has spent a life time writing and researching this subject. He concludes that there are1,239 in the O.T and 578 in the N.T. (1,817). Many have already been completed but the prophetic clock is still ticking. Every prophecy concerning Christ's first coming was fulfilled with precise accuracy. There is prophecy being fulfilled today and when Christ returns a second time there will be a programme of prophecy to be concluded. However, the focus of prophecy now concerns not Christ's validity but Muhammad's manipulative authority"

When one considers that Muhammad was a "prophet" it is surprising that the attention given to his "fulfilled prophecy" is relatively disproportionate to any other aspect of his ministry. An Egyptian academic, Jean al-Sadat, makes a colourful contribution to this area of the polemic. This scholar confidently comments, "There are at least 160 known and confirmed prophecies attributed to the Prophet Muhammad; which were fulfilled during and after his lifetime." Of course, we know that asking any kind of question or doubting such a person is likely to cause an uncivilised uproar. We have good reason to believe that there would be a theological earthquake measuring at least as great as the world record in Chile of 9.5 on the Richter Scale. This very vital question whether Muhammad was true or false is comprehensively covered by William Kilpatrick of Crisis Magazine. He successfully picks the bones and exposes the flesh.

We are covering old ground but we do this in order to introduce new territory.

Shay Muhammad Saalih reliably informs his readers that Muhammad began his "prophetic ministry" at the age of 25. The prophet's career could hardly be described as illustrious since he preached for almost 12 years and at the end of it had about 12 converts which were mostly made up of family members. This is unquestionably not something one would wish to have exhibited on their curriculum vitae. Muhammad's very first recorded "spiritual experience" was when he was in his mid-twenties and while he was wandering in the labyrinth of caves. It is traditionally purported by Muslims that he had an encounter with an angel (Bukhari 9.111). There is no convincing historical evidence to substantiate whether this meeting was angelic or demonic. Satan is known for being a chameleon – masquerading as an "Angel of Light." Out of ignorance Muslim's refer to the angel in the cave Hira as "The Archangel Gabriel." Since Michael is the only Archangel named in the Bible we can confidently rule out any rendezvous with an Archangel or Gabriel.

Muhammad's reaction to this mysterious meeting was not to dwell in the cave but to run in fear down the mountainside to find his wife, Khadija. She was a highly successful 40 year old business woman who ran a lucrative caravan-trading cartel. Her social standing meant that many in the tribe sought her advice. When Muhammad eventually met his wife, she became alarmed for he was saturated in sweat and breathless from running down the rugged rocks. At this time Muhammad was among a minority of Arabs of his day that were neither Jew nor Christian but monotheists, known as "Hanifs" (true believer). Khadija's cousin, Waraqa, was a well respected religious man who also happened to belong to the Hanif's. He was summoned to hear about the perspicacity in the cave and to give counsel to the still shaken Muhammad. It was no surprise that after hearing of the tumultuous events in the cave that he swallowed the story hook, line and sinker. From this point on Muhammad the keeper of camels would be "Muhammad the Prophet." This exchange heralded the beginning of Muhammad and the Quran and the Messenger and the Message. He would soon become the answer to every Arab's prayer.

Intriguingly, there is a prophet in the Old Testament that rivals Muhammad in the Quran. They have so much in common we could be forgiven for thinking they were related. Balaam (Numbers 22) was such a shameful and scandalous prophet that his reputation was ubiquitous. The etymology of his name is uncertain but he had the misfortune not to be an Israelite. He was an unscrupulous prophet who sold his services and fell head first into the pit that God commands we ardently avoid. He was a "lover of money" and that says the Lord, "Is the root of all evil" (1Timothy 6:10). The phoney prophet opposed God's people, the Israelites, and was used as a tool of the devil. Now all of this does sound remarkably familiar, Muhammad had a reputation that more than rivalled the Biblical false prophet. If ever there was a man with a love of riches then it was decadent Muhammad. A career in plundering and pillaging had left him in a covetous and prosperous state. The prophet became a notorious established lover of money overnight. It is reported that when he was not sleeping with one of his umpteen wives, he would sleep with his lucre. Not surprisingly, since Salaam and Muhammad followed false gods they too became disreputable false prophets. Dr. David Woods remarks, "Their only claim to fame was sheer shame."

It would be impossible to mention false prophets without alluding to the current day representatives. It is argued by many, including Father Jerome; Francis is one of the most discredited Pope's to ever breathe a breath. He shamefully appears in the top ten list of false teacher's found in "Christian" ministries. "Is the Pope a Catholic?" asks, Father Linus Clovis. The unholy father once claimed, "Jews can circumvent Christ and attain a degree of holiness without Him." We have heard this comment often but never so publicly and from a "priest." The number of false prophets has now reached saturation point. You only have to turn a corner or a page and there will be one waiting. What is pertinent in this work, is at the crux are two prominent prophets, Muhammad and Christ. Since they have a different belief system it automatically means they are vehemently opposed to one another. For example; Muhammad's command in the Quran is "kill the infidel" and Christ's commission in the Bible is "save the lost" (Religion of Peace). Allah is rumoured to be "merciful" but his holy book contains in excess of 100 violent verses all applicable for today.

Instinct and intuition says that it is highly unlikely that any person has asked aloud and lived, the question, "Is Muhammad a false prophet?" This happens to be the same sort of question that Muslim's mouth of Christ. Therefore, it is only reasonable to reciprocate and solicit Muhammad and Muslim's as to their authenticity. If the prophet proves false, that begs the question; what about the Qur'an and Allah? Are they fakes too? A brief glance over the shoulders will divulge a paradigm that academics have pursued when investigating this subject of false prophet. Captivatingly, the vast majority of scholars turn first to the word "prophet." Their argument centres on the validity of Muhammad's prophecies and so every prophecy is painstakingly assayed. Contrary to the academia who begin with the first word "false," we shall start with the last word "prophet."

What we do know is that Muhammad produced abysmal results as Islam's first and last so-called prophet. We have heard that his brief ministry in Mecca lasted over a decade and at the end, he had very little to show for it. All that Allah's prima donna prophet could achieve was a pocket full of naïve new converts. As far as the record goes these few were split between volunteers and the coerced; the latter being Islam's commonest form of proselytising. We are persuaded that since some were relatives of the prophet, that some conversions probably did transpire. What else leaves us sceptical is that prophets are appointed by God and not self-appointed as was Muhammad. There is the suggestion by a myriad of

The Bloody Religion of Peace

Muslim's that a total of 160 prophecies were made and fulfilled by "the last messenger." What makes the water more muddy is that these prophecies stretch across three sources, Qur'an, Hadith and Last Days Prophecies. According to Andrew Vargo the line in the sand between a prophecy and a statement is distended and indeterminate. If you believe Sheikh Dayyib, and we do not; he lists the essential qualities of a prophet as: forgiveness, good manners, gentleness, tender heart, generosity, concern for others and mercy to mankind. He then ascribes all these attributes to Muhammad. If Sherlock Holmes was given this description, it would not lead him to Muhammad but it would lead him on a wild good chase.

When Muhammad was not decapitating fellow Muslims he was busy crucifying Christians in the name of "The Bloody religion of Peace." The Quran mentions Jesus as a prophet (19:30 Yusif Ali) in a number of places but curiously never in the context of killing. What Dr. Charles Ryrie said when he was asked the difference between Muslim and Christian "regeneration," was shrewdly stated, "The former has a change of mind and the latter a change of heart." As we turn the pages of a Quran (English) we procure a plethora of texts that acknowledges Jesus in variegated forms but most are crudely misapplied. It has been casually promulgated by C.A.I.R. (Council American Islamic Research), a front for terror; that we regularly and repeatedly read that Muhammad and Muslims are "in" the Quran. Here lies the causatum. It is asserted by Spencer, "If Muslim's were not in the Quran but "in" Christ, how different the religious landscape would appear today."

When we pause to contemplate, it is highly inconceivable that this narrative will be well received in the Muslim community, and for that matter, in the Ecumenical Movement too, which includes amongst others; the apostate Anglican and Roman churches. Those who dare to reject the "truth" of Muhammad, are in essence dismissing Islam's "prince of prophets." The question on many more lips is whether Allah, who supposedly used Muhammad to write the Quran, is the same God who revealed Himself in the incarnation? One of the most common phrases is, "There is only one God." It is true – there is only one but which one do we mean? This question of "who is God" usually generates more heat than it does light. However, our attention is drawn to relevant exerts from the Bible that are made by author and apologist, Matt Slick (C.A.R.M.); "Who is a liar but he who denies that Jesus is the Christ? He is the Antichrist who denies the Father and the Son. Who is most clamorous in their denying that Jesus is the Christ? It is Islam. There is only one thing a blind person cannot do and that is see. Muslim's will remain blind as long as they reside in Islam.

According to John and the Bible, the spirit of Antichrist will not only denegate the written and spoken word of Christianity but will also deny the deity of Christ. But even worse it condemns any belief in the Son as a cardinal sin. Significantly, this is not sin in the normal sense, but the most fallacious kind of sin imaginable. The sin that God should be Father and Son is a anathema to Muslims. This core Christian belief is for all facets of Islam, an abomination – it is the greatest sin ever conceived! Of course, we know other religions such as the Jews and they deny the divinity of Christ. However, He is not part of their revelation and so Jews do not sense any necessity to believe Him. The point is that the Jews have not made Jesus as a central tenet of Judaism. Contrary to this, Muhammad appeared six centuries after Christ was born and one of his pivotal dogmas is the definitive denial of the Son-ship of Jesus. This is he fulcrum of Joel Richardson book "The Islamic Antichrist," which dismantles the theological structure of Islam and leaves it in ruin.

The eminent Dr. Daniel Pipes deduces, "While many religions and systems of belief exist that do not agree with the Christian doctrines; only Islam fulfils the role of a religion that exists to strenuously deny those biblical beliefs." It is awkward to square the scriptural evidence with the current trend that implies Islam and Christianity are distant cousins. We discover it is even more difficult when we try to reconcile it with the assertion that if we worship the same God and if that is true, then we must revere the same Jesus. Academia permanently procrastinate over this issue of which god is true or which way is right? If you meet a Muslim he will tell you that Muhammad says "follow me." (Quran 7:157). However, if you ask a Christian the same question, he will tell you that Jesus says, "I am the way, the truth and the life" (John14:6). Since both beliefs advocate following them; how do we determine which one is right? The two entities require us to go in a certain direction but since those directions are diametrically opposed, how on earth do we resolve which route to take? The decisive factor depends on the "compass" that is being used. Muslim's take the Quran as a their compass to guide them. Conversely, Christian's use their Bible. To reach the eternal desired destination depends on reading the right book and listening to the right voice. Essentially, the hinge on which eternity swings is knowing the author personally.

Allah, the great imposter, in pretending to be God has committed an horrendous sin. Alien to God is Allah who has perpetrated a terrible transgression in pretending to be the Creator God. We have false prophets today who play god but their actions are almost insignificant compared to the activities of Allah through the vehicle of Muhammad. We ought not to be surprised that Muhammad had one name in particular that will stick in our throat like a fish bone. He was inanely called the "prophet of peace." This title is inconceivable. There are some 25,000 words in the vocabulary of the average adult but the solitary word "peace" is extraneous to the prophet's own language.

It is incumbent that we take heed of the Lord's warning, "Beware of false prophets who... inwardly are ravenous wolves." The word "ravenous" seems a most suitable description for Muhammad. Torturing prisoners was second nature to the Tyrant. He would think nothing of castrating a prisoner while alive and then cramming the testicles in to the mouth of the poor victim. Women fared no better with wickedness abounding. The so-called prophet of peace would not hesitate to cut off their nipples or slicing off their finger tips while they were conscience. Muhammad raided caravans and fought battles. His blood lust continued with the massacre of a multitude of Jews (ROP). In spite of the historical precedence, Muslim's paint a picture of a passive prophet of peace. To calculate the exact number of people Muhammad murdered, is fraught with difficulty. He not only put the sword to Jews and Christians but also Muslims. A conservative number is that he butchered thousands. The same term, ravenous, could also be used to name his successors. Islam's 1400 year history is unquestionably written in blood with slaughter and subjugation shaping the Islamic landscape. Estimates vary but the consensus appears to be 2.7 million killed in the name of "The Bloody Religion of Peace," making Islam the most perverse and prolific murdering machine in the history of mankind. Muhammad's catalogue of atrocities make Stalin seem like a Sunday School Teacher.

Muslims believe they are said to be ridiculously sanctified by the blood of murdered kafirs, which is unlike Christians who are justified and sanctified only by the blood of Christ. If we do with Muhammad what a detective would do with a criminal and carry out a background check; we would be disgusted by the condemning evidence. Should Muhammad be alive today he would no doubt have a solitary seat sweating on death row, while waiting for his imminent execution. The list of offences committed by the prophet are both gross and ghastly. What we need to realise is that Muslims do not see these as crimes unless someone else is guilty of them. Muslim men obtain their moral code from Muhammad, so what the prophet did they can do. This is a condensed list of common crimes that Muhammad is on record as routinely rubber stamping.

- Assaulting and abusing his wife – six year old Aisha. This little girl was given the repulsive task of cleaning up the semen stains made by Muhammad. When she was a baby they would bath together so he could rub his penis over various parts of her body in masturbation. Being a man of "mercy" he was not obliged to consummate the marriage to his 6 year old child bride but tarried until she was aged 9. This can be substantiated by Quranic texts. We learn from this example and others that the prophet was unashamedly a seasoned paedophile.
- The sexual abuse of a little girl cannot be justified in any court unless Muhammad is the judge. Quranic passages were once changed, partly out of embarrassment and partly because they could not be coherently explained. Since a six year old little girl cannot be held responsible for being violated, Muhammad was additionally guilty of multitudinous random rapes.
- This "holy man" was so righteous that he raped a disabled woman. Later he murdered a woman and had sexual intercourse with the dead body. When he found his aunt dead he wasted no time in having sex with her in the grave in which she was placed. His depravity knew no end.

- All captured women were raped by him and he had a collection of sex slaves on call to meet his needs. He went on to have sex with sixty one women, many of whom he violently and viciously raped. The consensual argument that was bandied about fell flat on its face; sex with a child is not consensual. Raping children and women is not consensual. Forced anal sex with the spoils of war is not consensual. All the following incidents are aggravated acts of rape and not concordant sex:
- Muhammad's eleven wives, although some records say he had thirteen, were invariably abused and assaulted and of course, raped. Many of the women who were raped were defiled during menstruation and highly humiliated.
- He was preoccupied with beheading anyone who stood still long enough. This included boys who were first inspected for pubic hair. The decapitation infatuation continued at a pace with 600-900 Jewish men beheaded in one morbid massacre.
- The cult leader relished in all forms of torture; amputation, decapitation, castration, disembowelment and murder of Jews and Christians who were ruthlessly executed. Those who refused to convert promptly met a brutal and bloody demise.
- As a dictator overseeing a totalitarian regime he butchered people like you would kill cattle. One of his most hideous practices was immolation. The screams from the victims engulfed in the flames would wake the dead!
- He had an insatiable appetite for blood and this was manifested in his terrorising and torturing of kafirs. In addition to this the prophet instigated sixty massacres, including the twenty seven that he personally spearheaded.
- This wicked man man was an inveterate liar and this became an integral part of Islamic doctrine and culture which still persists today.
- The prophet married his daughter-in-law; approved multitudinous acts of prostitution and personally subjugated and violated an unknown number.
- As a "prophet of peace," he had a particular propensity for forcing wives to endure rape and a variety of perverse sexual performances,

in front of the women's husbands. Muhammad was convinced that wife beating was a sacred duty and so it was approved as a religious rite.
- The leader was actively involved in suicide attacks, executed apostates and dismembered homosexuals. The prophet was intensely savage and showed none of the mercy that he and Allah were rumoured to possess.
- His stoning of victims became ritualistic with hordes gathered to throw fist-sized stones at just about anyone who missed Muhammad's mark. It appears there was no limit to the number or the age.
- All of his favourite sermons were focused on death and were invariably filled full of hatred and poison, particularly for other religions where his hostility was relentless.
- Many forced conversions were performed with his sword and were obviously non-negotiable. Innumerable heads would be removed by those who dissented.

The verdict reached by the intelligentsia is that Muhammad was psychologically driven by a pathological necessity for supremacy. It is further postulated that Muhammad had a seared conscience and was speculatively beyond redemption. The abridged lengthy account that precedes this passage can be substantiated by reading the Hadith and Quran. If the above is overlooked, it is imperative that you do not neglect to read the Quran. After all, the pro-Islamic research group Quora informs us that there are a mere 114 chapters, 6236 verses and 77,449 words. This amounts to one tenth of the Bible which carries more weight and shines more light. The theologian Dwight Pentecost, maintains, "A diligent reader can complete the Quran in less than a day but the 765,000 words of the Bible will require 3 days (depending translation).

We have given the prophet much more grace here than he ever gave to anyone, anywhere. But it is only fitting that we conclude by excogitating something of his prophetic claims. The Quran portrays Muhammad as "The Seal of Prophets." This means for Sunni and Shia there can be no more prophets. Muhammad has slammed the door shut on any further revelation. Very interestingly, the Ahmadiyya Muslim's, which other Muslims perceive as heretical, are out of tune with Muhammadan's and would not see eye to eye. The largest population is found in Pakistan with over 4 million adherents. There are intrinsic differences between the Ahmadi's and Muslims but the kernel that distinguishes the two is Muhammad's role in eschatology. The Ahmadi's remarkably believe it will be Jesus and not Muhammad who spectacularly appears at the end of the age.

We would be remiss now, if we did not direct our attention specifically towards the "messenger of god." Muhammad had a number of names or titles attributed to him, but his actual name means "highly praised." He was widely regarded as an enigmatic individual who successfully seduced one fifth of the world to blindly follow him. Axiomatically, virtually all he ever said and did appears to be verified and some of the evidence is interestingly independent. Everything from his mundane birth to his reprobate life and degenerate death, is documented in detail. If we can believe Uqba ibn Mu'ayt, once a recognised mouthpiece for Muslim's; there is enough literature to fill the reputedly largest library in the world at Alexandria, with over 400,000 recorded documents. Shilman Fellow, Hugh Fitzgerald enunciates, "The totalitarian Islamist doctrine of Sharia mandates the spread of Islam by all believers and submission to its laws even by non-believers. Not all Muslims practice this, but those who do represent a major threat to the free world." (Hugh Fitzgerald).

When we consider the life of the "apostle of god," and his bloodthirsty catalogue of campaigns; we can elicit enough material to fill the cave at Hira with those accounts of Muhammad's despicable deeds. Antithetically, in his death there is insufficient documents and manuscripts to occupy even one single bookshelf. The death of a despot should be something to celebrate; not necessarily because he has died, but more importantly it means he cannot continue killing others. When Muhammad died the number of tears were few and far between. It was ironical that the person who killed him was from Khaibar. This was a strict Jewish tribe who Muhammad conquered by spilling their blood far and wide. The chief Jew of Khaibar, was a godly man called Kinana; who was barbarically beheaded and his beautiful wife Safiya was savagely taken captive by Muhammad.

The Jewess mourned day and night and during this time of sorrow she hatched a perfect plan to murder the monstrous man who had tortured her dear husband to death. Under great duress, Safiya was unceremoniously married to Muhammad. It was her resplendence that first caught Muhammad's eye and it was this same beauty that would bring about his devilish downfall. At supper, she would execute her ingenious ploy. All of her planning and plotting was about to be hatched. She knew most men preferred goat but for an unknown reason Muhammad chose lamb. It is necessary to digress for a moment. Muslim's inanely believe that eating pork is a egregious act for they maintain it will make them unclean. This is of course, a puerile position to adopt. Muhammadan's routinely and randomly commit sodomy, rape, and bestiality but apparently none of these capricious practices causes even a hint of defilement. No amount of pig can render a person unclean. If a man swallowed a whole pig; it would still be impossible to make him dirty or defiled. Typically, where the Quran is found wanting the Bible is not. "What goes in someone's mouth does not defile them, but what comes out of their mouth, that is what defiles the" (Matthew 15:11). Any thing that goes in the mouth will find its way to the stomach but in contrast and critically, what comes out of the mouth is from in the heart.

Safiya had worked hard preparing everything so the meal would be memorable. No one knew what was about to happen except Safiya. She was aware that Muhammad preferred lamb and so she placed the food down for them to eat and then withdrew. She watched and waited for her "husband" to pick-off a piece of "succulent" meat and he predictably chose the lamb. Almost immediately he knew that the meat was poisoned but it was too late. The last prophet had his last piece of lamb. Muhammad only had a mouthful which suggested his death would be protracted and agonising.

During his last days and even hours, Muhammad began to hallucinate and pray to the angel Gabriel. Why Gabriel is anyone's guess because she was not equipped to help him. Ibn Sa'd refers to this episode in the Hadith with the prophet pleading for healing. According to Ibn Sa'd the angel replied to Muhammad's cries, "Gabriel was chanting to him saying, "In the name of Allah I chant to ward off from you every thing that harms you and against every envier and from every evil eye and Allah will heal you." The wife of the prophet Aisha was heard to say, "in the name of Allah Who will cure You and who will heal you from every malady." It emerged that the chants and cries fell on deaf ears and went unheard. Muhammad was found in the most unenviable place – "a man without faith, hope or love. This is a godless position.

Strangely, Safiya was able to see the same excruciating torment in Muhammad that she witnessed in her first husband. For three days Muhammad lay prostrate convulsing and defecating and before darkness fell, he passed from this life in to the next one. The prophet only had "three possibilities." He did not die a martyr's death so any sight of "paradise" under Islam was obscured. He was not born again by the Spirit of God so the gates of heaven stayed shut. The third and last choice is unthinkable and is called hell. The list of Muhammad's criminality exceeds the length of the Blue Nile. He was guilty of breaking all of his own laws as well as many others. The only guarantee left was a place of everlasting punishment. Where is Muhammad today? It is only God who knows the end from the beginning but if he died as he lived then he is in hell. We can be completely confident of that because no narcissist, hedonist, paedophile, murderer, terrorist, adulterer, rapist, madman, torturer, assassin, misogynist, thief or heathen, will ever have a home in heaven.

It is generally accepted that the scientist Thomas Edison invented the first light bulb. He was also renowned as the world's greatest inventor with 1,093 patents! What half the world does not realise is that the claim of inventing the first light bulb was bogus and nothing more than a myth. The truth is that Edison made only the filament that sits inside the bulb. There are those who would adduce that Muhammad was a philanthropic prophet. What half of the world do not realise is that the claim of being benign was bogus and merely another myth. The fact is that Muhammad courted death and destruction; war and not peace. This is the man who has been described historically as a dictator and despot. However, it would appear that there is another Muhammad. Someone has unearthed or resurrected, a reformed meek and mild character who would not hurt a fly. Unfortunately, the reformers have only contemned the written records. When we turn to the Hadith we find in various places that the prophet of

Islam said, "I have been called to fight all men until they testify that there is no god but Allah and Muhammad is His messenger" (*faith al-Bari*). There are two famous motto's. One we should grasp and one we should release. Muhammad's motto reads like this, "The goal of Islam is the rule of Sharia" On the other side of the coin is the motto of General de la Billiere, "If you want peace prepare for war."

One of many examples that robustly refutes the myth that Muhammad preferred peace over war was when he heard of a man called Usayr ibn Zarim who was gathering a force to oppose the Muslims. According to the true story (ibn Ishaq/Hisham) of what happened, Muhammad sent an armed band to Usayr's community, which convinced him that he would be guaranteed a safe passage to a meeting with Muhammad to discuss peace. Zarim was sincerely interested in a congenial exchange, so the leader and his thirty men trusted Muhammad's word. All the men went unarmed with peace on their agenda. However, much to their surprise and horror they were all summarily slaughtered by the marauding Muslims.

Another notorious and well-documented episode is the series of events leading up to the massacre of the Meccan's by the Muslim army in 630. The Muslim's were first to break the treaty, the first to attack and the first to draw blood. All this carries the hall marks of "The Bloody Religion of Peace." The leader of the Meccan's Abu Sufyan, suspecting that trouble was brewing; decided to journey to Medina to speak with Muhammad concerning establishing a modicum of peace. After speaking casually to some Muslims who were pitched outside the main camp, he eventually met Muhammad who immediately rebuffed his unconditional offer of a peace plan. To rub salt in Sufyan's wounds, he unceremoniously dismissed him and sent him packing. The so-called man of "peace" then returned to hatching his plan of bloodshed.

When Abu Sufyan saw them marching to his city he made one more desperate attempt to deter Muhammad. So despairing was the man that he engaged the help of Muhammad's wife to make intercession for him. The woman attempted to dissuade her husband but her advances were futile. His mind was made up and he was determined to defeat Mecca. Once the killing started there was nothing anyone could do. Muhammad believed that by killing kafir's it was possible to avoid hell. It is indeed possible to avert hell but it is not Muhammad's way. The prophet was knocking on the wrong door and believing the deluded dogma buried in the Quran (19:70, 4:95). This text leaves one believing the avoidance of hell is a reality. The Pope and the Roman church have adopted the same duplicitous diatribe. Every Quran (Sura 69, 84:7) instructs the Muslim to believe that they will go to hell for their sins but after paying a "fine" they are released to enter paradise. (There is no mention which currency is acceptable!). Nevertheless, the proposition is that the only cast iron guarantee of being propelled to paradise is through Jihad (Quran 3:169, 9:39). The logic behind this ultimatum is seriously warped. If a Muslim kills a kafir in battle, the kafir takes the Muslim's place in hell. This is patently not an inspired creed but is another fragile fabrication procreated by Islam.

The hypothesis that the residuum of Muhammad's finger prints were found on the "holy text" is an extortionate and extravagant speculation. Such a suggestion is a half-baked cake and lacks substance. This can be explained by virtue of the fact that when Muhammad was aged 40 in the year 610, he sauntered in to a claustrophobic cave called "*Hira*" (a girls name meaning the hill) and was miraculously greeted by the Angel Gabriel. Many Arabic scholars make the same elementary mistake of saying it was the "Arch-angel Gabriel", but there is only one Archangel named in the Bible and that is Michael. Meanwhile, it was Gabriel who allegedly instructed Muhammad with an oral message from god. The secular history books make much of the verity that Muhammad was unable to read or write. An illiterate person, can listen but they cannot use the medium of literacy or numeracy. This indicates that Muhammad's illiteracy; as the academics stringently state, meant he was obviously unable to record the message given by Allah to Gabriel or anyone else. This leaves Muhammadan's stuck in the mud. It is inconceivable that god would choose an illiterate figure to be his prima face "prince of prophet's," and a mouthpiece to sound out the oracles of the Islamic god.

We are frequently exposed to Islamic claims that they are the largest and fastest growing religion. There is no objective consensus that this statement is waterproof and accurate. Naturally, no Muslim will tell you differently but if you carefully consider the fact that many conversions to Islam are in fact coercions, you will arrive at a different destination. Add to this the repeated reports of multitudes fleeing from Islam, then one suspects there are far fewer Muslim's than Islam engenders. This brings to mind a mother of four in an African village who was given an ultimatum; accept Allah or have her breasts sliced off. She rejected Allah because she had accepted Christ. Four men held her down and the Jihadist cut off each breast. There is an oft offered Quranic (2:256) verse that stipulates, "let there be no compulsion in religion." Of all the lies that Muhammad manufactured this makes one of the most fraudulent. The distance between Sura 2 and Sura 9 is not great but the meaning of the progressive narrative is huge. Contradictions and abrogations abound. These two devices "deceive" and "defeat" are applicable against the infidel. The deception of not being compelled to embrace Islam (Quran 2:256, 10:99) is later effaced with the threat of "slay the idolaters" (Quran 9:5, 8:12). Like everyone else, "The Bloody Religion of Peace," may have had a conscience but if it did it became submerged inside the Islamic swamp.

There are many knots in Islamic ideology that are regularly expostulated. However, more ink has been spilled over Muhammad's articulacy than any other Islamic topic. What is intriguing is that the number adopting a defensive role for Muhammad far outweigh those who assertively oppose him. The academia today, take a conservative line when it comes to Muhammad's language deficiencies. Most Islamic commentators adopt a predictable stance to defend him but the variation is as wide as problematic Pakistan. One of the writer's who appropriates a guarded role is Abdulrahman Khan. He argues that there were innumerable illiterate people at this time so it holds no significance that Muhammad may have been one of them. Ahlul Bayt makes the comment that Muhammad received "divine inspiration" and therefore was not illiterate. Although, there was a time when Muhammad could only "mark" his name; Ajsad Jaleel purports, "Muhammad became a businessman and was surely given inspiration." All these perspectives carry some credence but none of them carry any real weight. It is reasonably argued by the Ahmadi Muslim sect that if one was a prophet from god and sent to the people of god; written and spoken language would be an absolute necessity. Allah settles and seals the matter with this telling text; "Those who follow the messenger; the Prophet who can neither read nor write, whom they will find described in the Torah and Gospel (which are) with them" (Quran 7:157). In complete confutation Allah dismisses all the Islamic apologists and scholars, by confirming the Prophet of god could not read or write any more than he could walk on water!

We are afflicted today, not with a murderous Muslim who could not read and write but with one who does not read and write the Bible. It is somewhat gauling that the Ambassador and Mayor of multicultural London, is as ignorant of the English Language Book, as Anjem Choudary is disparaging of the country that meets all his needs, This is of course nothing new for there has always been reprobates in every era, When we consider the present and not the past; it is not of any tremendous surprise that the man with the responsibility of managing the "Capital City of Europe" is none othere than a Muslim. Such an appointment is as absurd as making Abu Hamza al-Masri Governer of H.M.P. Belmarsh Prison, We learn that large swathes of the public have nothing but contempt for Sadiq Khan the mayor of London who is also reviled. He is infamous for stating "He stands on the Quran." This immediately tells us that his loyalties are to Islam and his allegiance is not to London. As a Muslim he has a contrived agenda which allows him to say one thing and do another. Since becoming Mayor he has played it fast and loose, with all major crime figures increasing (Raheem Kassam). Just about every conceivable felony from rape (up 18.3%) to robbery (up 33.4%) has risen faster than the American F14 Tomcat. We can safely say that Mr. Khan was not appointed for his competency for office. On the contrary, he was appointed because he was a Muslim who will most certainly mirror his role model; the prophet Muhammad. It is well documented by Kameel Nasr that Khan's habit of wearing white shirts do nothing to conceal the stains on his character. His nexus with flagitious groups such as Fatah and Al-Aqsa are condemning. The writing was on the wall for Muhammad but he could not read and write. The same words are on the wall for Khan and he can read and write. It has been suggested that Sadiq Khan will one day become the greatest disaster since the Black Death Pandemic of 1347 which saw 3.5 million men women and children buried or burned.

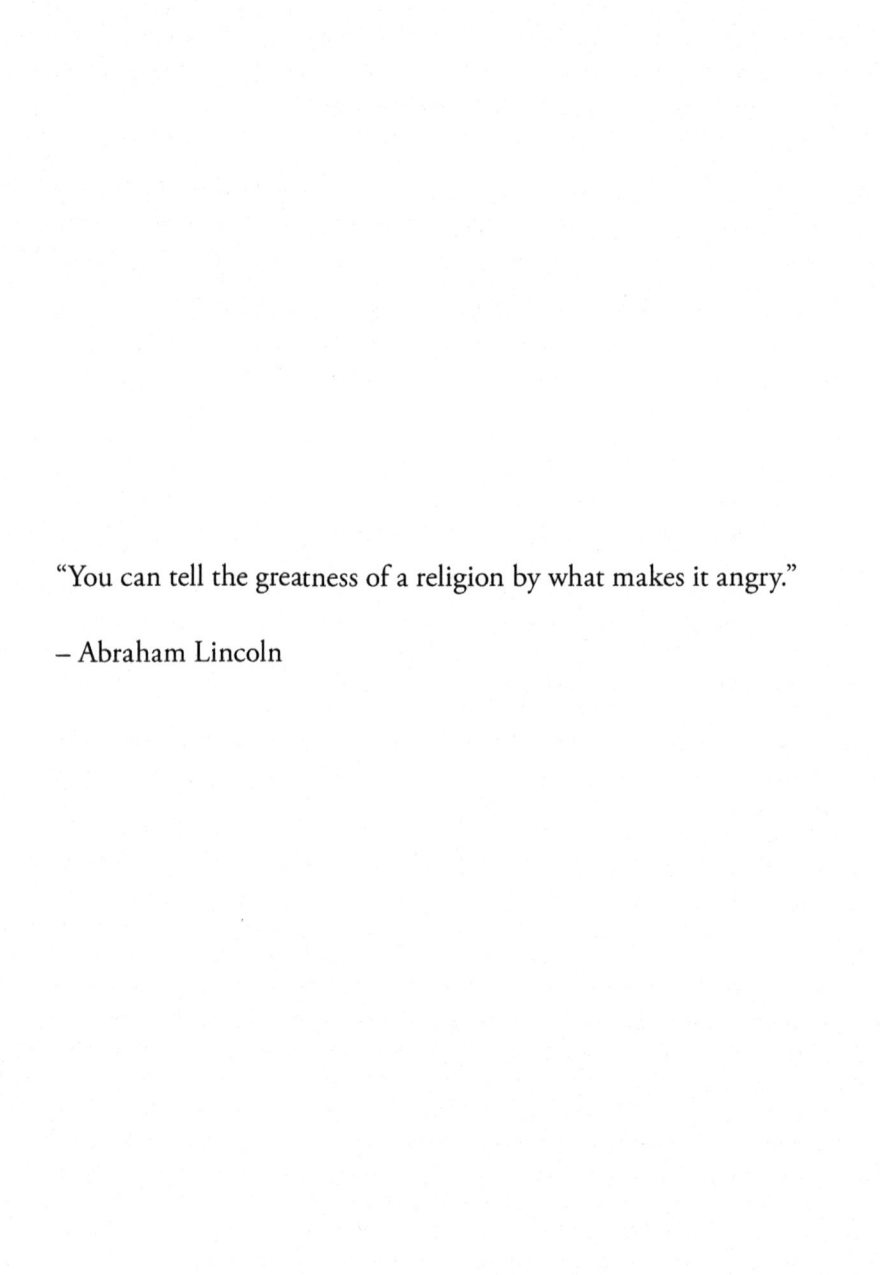

"You can tell the greatness of a religion by what makes it angry."

– Abraham Lincoln

Chapter Three

Quran

"The Quran is an accursed book. So long as there is this book there will be no peace in the world."

- Max Webb

If you happen to be one of the billion Muslim's in the world then you will hold the Quran in high esteem as the Islamic "holy book." Since the author of the book is allegedly, Allah, it is purported to be perfect to the point of being irreproachable. It is suggested that the book has retained its integrity, since it was orally transmitted to Muhammad, by none other than Allah. Should this be a fact and not fiction, we would expect the entire text to be faultless or flawless. Thanks to Daniel Greenfield of the Horrowitz Centre, we are reminded by him that Muslim's are predisposed to live more by fear than faith. This juxtaposition causes those who subscribe to Islam to refrain from daring to question what is written or said. Muslim's just simply do not have that freedom or liberty to challenge what Allah supposedly spoke or wrote. They appear content to accept scripture not inspirationally but speculatively. There is a clarion congruity here between both the Roman Catholic and Muslim, in that both belief systems accept what the priest, or imam says without confirming it in the "sacred texts." This practice has been commonly carried out for two reasons. Firstly, it ensures that the power is not in the pews but remains in the pulpit. Secondly, the issue of control is exercised by the clergy who can divulge and disseminate as little or as much of the scriptures that their fancy takes them.

If you are named or known as a Muslim, the Quran is your austere rule book or "Holy Writ." The Quranic scriptures and the author, Allah, are considered by many to be the personification of perfection. All Muslim's are recognised through the indelible label they wear called Islam. We read in the Quran; the words of Allah: "This day have I perfected your religion for you and completed my favour upon you and have chosen for you Islam as your religion" (Quran 5:3). Allah, himself, has declared or decreed that he is sublime and supreme. In the retail clothing market the label attached to the garment is important because it can disclose its commercial worth. The Islamic label that is found on every Muhammadan also demonstrates a sense of value in the sight of god. The label perfection comes from the author who it is claimed to be, no other than Allah. We are reminded by Brigitte Gabriel that Islamic sources say "god transmitted these words orally to Muhammad." If these statements are true and the god Allah participated in penning the pages of the Qur'an, then one would expect it to be from any solecism. Unlike Christians who believe God and then see, Muslims demand to see before they will believe. This is no doubt why journalist Caroline Glick of the Jerusalem Post explicates; Muslim's spend their entire lives "trying" while in contrast, Christian's spend it trusting.

One of the major sticking points within the Quran and of course, with Muslim's too; is the plethora of contradictions found folded in its pages. These variances have been well documented and accredited by apologist's such as Dr. William Craig and the former atheist Lee Strobel. The contradictions by Allah and Muhammad are like a trumpet call sounding out to anyone who has ears to hear. This disclosure of errancy divulges that both Muhammad and Allah are fallible and therefore, unreliable. Their exposure leads us to believe that they have clay feet and cannot stand up to any serious scrutiny. The number of chapters or Sura's that contain contradictions is questionable. There seems to be no consensus concerning exact numbers but those who agree to the Quran being flawed with discrepancies are multitudinous. There are a collection of contradictions that surface frequently and because they carry more weight they are used more often. Take for example Sura 19:67 that states that "man was created out of nothing." However, in Sura 15:26 we learn that "man was created out of clay." Matt Click (CARM) makes a valid point, "Since clay is something, we have a contradiction since "nothing" excludes the possibility of "clay." What is remarkable about this subject of Quranic authenticity, is that there are some fringe Muslims who are bold enough to contradict their own religious book. Take for instance the view of Ali Sina, a "conservative" Muslim who devoted much of his time filtering the Quran for error. Quite astonishingly he stopped counting the mistakes when he reached 1000! A sceptical international Islamic preacher, Naik Zakir, who is naturally respected by Muslims, dismisses outright all of these questionable verses. In response Christine Williams says of Naik, "Dr. Zakir's pedagogy does not measure up under the theological microscope." What Dr. Naik sets out to achieve is to repudiate every error in the Quran through the means of abrogation. We have crossed this bridge before and in its simplest sense it means any question or contention can conveniently be brushed aside and nullified.

When excogitating the Islamic scriptures, the very first issue to strike us is the dissonance of the Quran. After reading, and one must read the whole book; we stumble on at least 109 verses that are not just violent but vicious. This is astounding since Allah is portrayed as all merciful in the very same book. When confronting the Quran we find it riddled with endless savagery, that Muslim's feebly attempt to denounce. Their tactic is to immediately go on the defensive and resort to quoting, "...the Lord is is merciful..." (Sura 6147). There are some cogent clauses in the Quran that also need to be accentuated. Firstly, the Quran is thematically inconsistent and chronologically crippled. Perhaps one of the leading Islamic authorities today, Arthur Jefferey, ought to comment here. He is emphatic when he states that the "sacred scriptures" in the Quran are unique, in that they petition and promote the "doctrine of abrogation." The Haifa University professor, Dr. David Bukay, a distinguished exegete of the Quran, questions the authorship. His findings are not in any way nebulous but are crystal clear. Rather surprisingly, but also pleasingly, is the titillation of Abu Mohammed Ali Ibn Ahmad Ibn Hazim, a celebrious commentator on Islamic works. His synopsis is two-fold. One, there is a flimsy denial within Islam that abrogation was being currently employed and two, exegete's were noticeably selective in the tried and tested texts being routinely addressed.

It will be profitable to remind ourselves that the word Quran means "recitation" and comprises of a series of so-called revelations that Muhammad claimed to have received from Allah at various and on convenient occasions. Similar to other religious books the Quran is divided into chapters and verses which are referred to as *"Sura's"* and *"Ayats."* When reading the 114 Sura's it becomes immediately apparent that they contradict the claim of being "perfectly arranged." Raymond Ibrahim draws attention to the fact that rather than being organised and ordered the Sura's and Ayats are oddly arranged according to "size." Since there is an absence of any chronological form, there is no continuity throughout the book. It may surprise readers to learn that the Quran was anthologised after Muhammad's death from a variety of materials subsumed from papyrus leaves, wood carvings, and animal bones. In addition to this Muhammad would often share his thoughts with his companions who were frequently being killed in Islam's bloodthirsty onslaught. It is well documented, asserts Pamela Geller, "The Quran is riddled with conjecture and contradiction; which Muslims exploit to tamper with texts or to cover with a coat of abrogation." This last word will resonate with many as the repeated random practice of utilising the later verses to obviate the early ones.

It is generally accepted that the words in the Muslim religious book are said to be that of Allah who literally communicated them directly to Muhammad. If this is true then the compilation of the book is unintelligible at best and incomprehensible at worst. The inconsistencies, diatribes, myths and literary bankruptcy, all strip bare any exhortation that the Quran is divinely authoritative. Of course, we have the availability and assistance of external sources like the Hadith (Muhammad's words and deeds), yet even when reading and grappling with this, we are still fraught with difficulty. The academic community concede that the earliest translations make for better assimilation, since the more modern versions have a habit of omitting grammatical inflections such as vowels and nouns. Scholars suspect that early transcripts have been either destroyed or disappeared, which means much of the true meaning of the words were long lost in the passage of time.

In this chapter we detect a storm starting to brew but it is not a storm in a teacup. In an effort to overcome their fragility, Muslim's do what they do best; Islam verbally and vehemently goes on the attack. The narrative goes something like this; "There is much more violence in the Old Testament than there is in the Quran." If you have ever found yourself on the receiving end of such a remark and have been caught off guard, then it is likely you were left stammering to find a rebuttal. Those who dry up and have nothing to say have usually forgotten the fundamental principle of exegetics. The golden rule of interpretation is to approach the passage in its context and setting. When scanning the OT and the "violent verses" we discover they are not current but historical. This cannot be said of the Quran, for their murderous texts are pertinent and applicable today. If we open the Quran we find a flood of poisonous passages pouring out that postulate; "Slay the unbelievers or infidels wherever you find them" (Quran 2:191). We can say with certainty that unbelievers are all those who fall in to the category of non-Muslim. Another Quranic passage predicates, "Slay the Jew and Christian." Many things can be said about Islam and the Quran but the overriding message is that Islam and peace is antithetical. In light of the mountain of written evidence, the only conclusion that a sober person might come to is that "Islam" is accurately rendered as "submission." and this is the correct Arabic linguistic expression as found in the "holy book" (Quran 9:30).

Should you be one of the growing groups of people, like the Palestinian Leader Mahmoud Abbas, who believe the Quran should win the Nobel Prize for peace; then you also probably think the world is flat! To say that the Quran is a bloodthirsty book would be the understatement of the century. There are in fact scores of vitriolic verses that urge Muslims to seek and slaughter all unbelievers. The reader finds that it is a normal custom in Islam to chop off heads, hands and feet. Of course, the depth of their depravity and degradation knows no end. Slitting the throat, cutting off genitals, disembowelling captives while they are still alive and gouging out the eyes of the "enemy" when they remain fully conscious, are all met with a Quranic gold seal of approval. Such is the depraved nature of the book that the author is essentially incontrovertibly devoid of any compassion. It is between such lines of contradiction that we repeatedly read that the Islamic god is "Allah Most Merciful." This self-acclamation of mercy amounts to one of the greatest statements of hypocrisy to ever fall from the mouth of man. The above wicked acts are merely a typical praxis of the commonest crimes against humanity that "The Bloody Religion of Peace," called Islam, casually commit on a daily basis.

Of all the religious books in the world, the Quran is unique. This is the only book that compels its adherents to declare a blood-lust war on all unbelievers or non-Muslims. They qualify that deposition not because of any hostility toward them but purely because they are as Geller rightly says, "savages!" One does not have to look very far before discovering the Quran is nothing more than a "manifesto for war." We read for instance, "O prophet strive hard against the unbelievers and the hypocrites, and be firm against them. Their abode is hell, an evil refuge indeed" (Sura 9:73). To "strive hard" in Arabic is the same idiom as *jihadi,* a verbal form of the renowned jihad. This striving was intended in the context of the battlefield. "When you meet the unbelievers on the battlefield, strike off their head and, when you have laid them low, bind your captives low, bind your captives firmly" (Sura 47.4). This sentiment is echoed time and time again, "O ye who believe! Fight the unbelievers who gird you about, and let them find firmness in you: and know that Allah is with those who fear him" (Sura 9:123).

The recipients of this warfare were those who rejected Islam and also those who professed faith but that is all they did. "Prophet, make war on the unbelievers and the hypocrites and deal vigorously with them. Hell shall be their home: so fight ye against the friends of Satan" (Sura 4:76). "Then, when the sacred months have passed, slay the idolaters wherever ye find them, and take them captive, and besiege them, and prepare for them each ambush. But if they repent and establish worship and pay the poor-due, then leave their way free. Lo! Allah is forgiving, merciful" (Sura 9:5). The meaning of the term "poor-due" here is *zakat* (payment), which is a cardinal command for Muslim's. Thus the verse is demonstrating that those idolaters who conform and keep to Islam shall be left alone to live "freely." Jews and Christians were also regarded as "idolaters" and were to be on the bruising end of Allah's fist. "Fight those who believe not in Allah nor the Last Day, nor hold that forbidden by Allah and His messenger, nor acknowledge the religion of Truth, (even if they are) of the people of the book, until they pay the *jizya* (Muslim tax levied only on non-Muslims) with willing submission, and feel themselves subdued" (Sura 9:29).

Of the 6000 or more verses in the Quran, Quora (social media) reminds us that some 164 are what is referred to as Jihad (holy war) texts. Islamic so-called exegetical's bend over backwards and cajole people in to believing jihad means an inward "struggling" or "striving." It is unscrupulous of any Muslim "scholar" to interpret jihad in any way other than in the context of "warfare." To suggest it is a "holy" war or "holy" struggle simply insults the intelligence of all the onlookers. In employing the adjunct "holy," David Woods espouses that this is another failed attempt "to pull the wool over our eyes." From a non-Muslim perspective, it would be exceedingly costly to underestimate the resolve of a Muslim who operates with a carte blanche modus operandi. Therefore, it should prove obvious that it is the utmost duty of every Muslim to comply "religiously" with the Quran, or ultimately, be cut off and even cut up! If one held any doubts about this, then the following imperative will quickly dismiss them. "Do ye make the giving of drink to pilgrims, or the maintenance of the Sacred Mosque, equal to the pious service of those who believe in Allah and the Last Day, and strive with might and main in the cause of Allah (*jihad fi sabil Allah*), with their goods and their persons, have the highest rank in the sight of Allah: they are the people who will achieve salvation" (Sura 9:19-20). This insidious Islamic theology, jihad fi sabil Allah (In the cause of Allah) points particularly to taking up arms for the sake of Islam and the purpose of war. This is a definitive text that can stand alone, unsupported, and without any reproach.

The pledge of paradise is a certainty as far as Muslim's are concerned. "To all those who 'slay and are slain' for Allah: "Allah hat purchased of the believers, their persons and their goods; for theirs (in return) is the garden (of paradise): they fight in His cause, and slay and are slain: a promise binding on Him in truth" (Sura 9:111). A myriad of Arabs have attempted to spiritualise these verses but have faltered and failed. The historical record and the climate of the context, leaves us in no doubt that Muhammad's intention was literal. It is not a coincidence that Muhammad (Allah) used a sword to scribe the scriptures. The DNA of the prophet, as found in the

Hadith and Quran is coloured scarlet-red. One needs to dig deep into the Quran to find anything remotely resembling peace. Some concede, such as Dr. Pipes, that there are a few "snowflakes" on several pages but it is a book predominantly filled full of blizzards to blast the unsuspecting infidel (non-Muslim). The theologian Alder Tozer propounds, "For the Muslim peace is neither plausible or palatable." He firmly believed, "The essence of peace is the absence of war." We can clarify and confirm with certainty; no traces of lasting peace have ever been detected on the Muslim moral radar.

The pacifist, James Law, pointedly pronounces, "Why would any open-minded person expect even a modicum of peace today when the last 1400 years has seen Islam slaughtering men, women and children?" Peace for the Muslim is viewed as a weakness and not a strength. Many know that Winston Churchill was a former Prime Minister of the United Kingdom but only relatively few are aware he held the Nobel Peace Prize for Literature. If any man is qualified to comment on the psychopathic anatomy of Islam, it is Winston Churchill. In his acclaimed book, The River War, Churchill devoted episodes to this sore subject of Muslim murder and mayhem. His most celebrated quotation remains tailor-made, "What the horn is to the rhinoceros and the sting is to the wasp, the Muhammadan's are to the world." Churchill was a seasoned army officer who crossed swords and drew blood battling Muslim tribes. At the end of his campaigns, Captain, Edward, George, Spencer-Churchill wrote, "Encountering Ideological Islam was eye opening and life changing. The only solution I see to this marauding menace of savages (Islam) is that we take no prisoners." Remarkably, the prison population in the U.K. is inching towards 90,000, with over 15% or 12,000, being Muslim. It is significant that half of this number are what Prison Studies label as virulent Pakistani and Somali nationals. In the U.S.A. those incarcerated is a staggering 2.2 million and climbing, with almost 200,000 being Muslim; states the quango Statista. Churchill's bold solution of no prisoners once curried countless backing. Intriguingly, Ryan Mauro of Clarion voices a similar sentiment today with the advocation of an expedient repatriation en masse. He elaborates further with the following comment, "It is not possible to remove the terrorist from the Muslim but it is possible to remove the Muslim from a country."

"Say: O believers! I worship not that which ye worship: nor worship ye that which I worship. And I shall not worship that which ye worship. Nor will ye worship that which I worship. Unto you your religion, and unto me my religion" (Sura 109:1-6). There is also diatribe for Muslim's not to engage in debate or disagree with unbelievers. "And dispute ye not with the people of The Book, except which means better (than mere disputation), unless it be with those of them who inflict wrong (and injury): but say, "We believe in the revelation which has come down to us and in that which came down to you; Our god and your god is one; and it is to him we bow" (Sura 29:46). Muslim's sincerely believe Islam teaches there is one god and that Allah of the Quran and the God of the Bible are the same god. Unfortunately, you can be sincere – sincerely wrong and mortally, Muslim's are. Many commentators, Christian and Muslim, stumble over the same stone. There is the inclination or tendency, which announces and accepts that Allah is dead but this supposition is highly problematic. For the god of Islam to have died he would obviously had to have lived. In light of the consensus amongst scholars of Islamic jurisprudence (Joseph Shacht, Norman Anderson, David Pearl and Christopher Melchert), who all resolutely reiterate that Allah was only alive in the imagination of Muhammad and his minion's. Like it or not, Allah was a heathen god who never breathed a breath – not one! For fourteen centuries men have been duped in to believing that Allah was god. This lie and a lie is a fabrication of the truth, has succeeded in standing the passage of time; only to bamboozle and brainwash billions of Islamic adherents.

A bizarre belief but one in which Muhammad believed; was the possibility of avoiding the horror of hell. This dogma or doctrine is overloaded with controversy. In essence, all this amounts to is just another myth from Muhammad the master of mythology. We should not be alarmed or surprised that the source of this directive is planted in the Quran (19:70, 4:95). This leaves one believing the possible avoidance of hell as a reality. The Pope and the Roman church have adopted a similar duplicitous discussion named purgatory. Every Quran (Sura 69, 84:7) instructs the Muslim to believe that he will go to hell for his sins but after paying (The currency is unknown!) a "get out clause," there is the likelihood of being released to enter paradise. It is quite extraordinary that 78.9% (Clarion) of

Muslim's fail to read their "holy book" but will be belligerently dogmatic when it comes to defending doctrines such as heaven and hell. We also ascertain there is purported to be a "cast iron guarantee" for a Muslim being propelled to paradise through the vehicle of Jihad (Quran 3:169, 9:39). The logic behind this ultimatum has its source sunk in Islamic scripture." If a Muslim kills a kaffir (infidel) in jihad, the kaffir takes the Muslim's place in hell. This hideous scenario could only be played out on the pages of what is becoming increasingly known as the "Unholy Book." The Quran has been referred to as a "bankrupt book" by Hugh Fitzgerald. His reason for stating that it is so impoverished is due to the Quran being devoid of any ethical or moral value. We would be derelict in our duty if we left the reader supposing such a spurious synopsis was a reality. As alarming as it is, there are no diversion signs on the road leading straight to hell. Contrary to the polemic of other religions, Raymond Ibraham paints a plain picture of the Christian perspective related to eternity; "Whether we go to heaven or hell does not concern what we have done in this life but rather what we have neglected to do."

It is highly pertinent that we make mention of the fact that the Quran does not end exactly as it began. The earlier passages when Muhammad was in Mecca, are much more propitiatory. We are imputed by Muslim's that they should not force a non-Muslim to accept Islam: "Let there be no compulsion in religion: truth stands out clear from error: whoever rejects evil and believes in Allah hath grasped the most trustworthy handhold, that never breaks" (Sura 2:256). This petulant text omits to say that Muslim's should not strive to subjugate those of The Book and make them pay the *jizya* (Tax/bribe-Sura 9:29). Of course, the truth is the opposite and is decidedly different with the disobedient, apostates and unbelievers, all being systematically and sacrificially slaughtered. The pages of the Quran are splattered with the blood drops of those who did not toe the line and bow the knee to Allah. From beginning to end, the landscape of this irreligious textbook is littered with human debris. Many believe that Islam cannot sink lower or become any worse but they would be radically wrong in their estimation. Modern Day Muslims have turned Mein Kampf in to a best seller and Adolf Hitler in to their elated hero. Islam has achieved the unthinkable and unknowingly done precisely what the Biblical prophet predicted, "Woe unto them that call evil good, and good evil" (Isaiah 5:20).

The work of ancient Islamic historians such as Ibn Ishaq and the contemporary commentator Abdullah al-Harari have been instrumental in influencing Islamic theologians to do as we have discussed and divide the Quran in to the "Meccan" and "Medinan" eras. As we turn the pages and progress through the Quran we are immediately struck by the escalation in bloodletting. The so-called "Religion of Peace" in Mecca expeditiously becomes "The Bloody Religion of Peace" in Medina. This transpiration was implemented by the megalomaniac Muhammad. After he turned his back on Mecca and his face to Medina, it is noticeable that the tone of his language was more belligerent and bellicose. The prophet turns up the temperature and becomes much more incendiary in his behaviour. We discern that the Medina texts are far deeper cutting than the milder Meccan writings. Muhammad had now indubitably adopted a more malevolent stance and the fruit of that is seen in the rivulets of blood. Theologians tend to distinguish dates in the sura's by the length of the language used. The Meccan vocabulary borders on containing pleasing poetic pieces that were perceptibly written by hand in ink. However, the Medinan pages consisted of dark and depressing copious commands to jihad warfare, and were undeniably written with blood and not ink.

At this confluence we are required to ask ourselves a pressing question, "Why does the geographical distinction matter to Muhammad – what is the importance of the Meccan and Medinan episodes?" It matters greatly because of the previously adduced Islamic doctrine of abrogation (*naskh*). What this alludes to is that Allah can change his mind like the wind changes direction. Muhammad commenced his journey in Mecca but by the time he arrived at Medina his scriptures had changed and so had he. The following sentence, or text, illustrates one of a number of discrepancies, We read in the Quran Sura 2:106, "None of Our revelations do We "abrogate" or cause to be forgotten, but We "substitute" something better or similar: knowest thou not that Allah Hath power over all things." If Allah has power over "all things" that must include the sanctioning of abrogation and the changing of the Quran. It also throws in to question the supremacy of Allah – if he was so supreme, or sovereign, there would be no necessity to "doctor" or concoct the completed so-called "Holy Book." The latter shift from moderate manuscript to vitiated verses, did not have Allah's finger prints but Muhammad's. With regard to this idea, the potent passages of Sura 9, including the infamous Sura 9:5 and the sword, all abrogate any allusion of peace penned previously. Writer Ali bin Ahmad believed Muhammad showed signs of suffering from a personality disorder which might explain why his character would veer from solemn to savage. The conclusion we come to is the Quran is absolutely arbitrary and could have been randomly reconstructed by Muhammad's manipulative hands.

What is it that makes the Quran so distinctly different to any other religious book in the world? It is the only "sacred writings" that declares war and demands death for unbelievers. Just in case there was any doubt in the Muslim mind, Allah has penned over one hundred vicious verses exhorting believers to wage war or Jihad against infidels. "When you meet unbelievers in the battlefield, strike off their heads..." (Sura 47:4). Such verses are by no means rare; they are regularly repeated. "O ye who believe! Fight the unbelievers who gird you about, and let them find firmness in you: and know that Allah is with those who fear Him" (Sura 9:123). The "all-merciful" Allah did not leave even the faintest of fissures in his stone hard doctrine, which meant not one single drop of mercy could ever permeate. The "prophet" would go on to unleash an unrestrained savagery in warfare that was so vile it caused his own followers to convulse. His animosity was to be directed against anyone and everyone who rejected the god of the Qur'an. What is sententious today is that one thousand four hundred years after Muhammad and nothing has changed. Men, women and children, who do not choose to follow the Islamic false faith, are dealt the direst death imaginable. Maulana was tired. She had shuffled along the dusty street of her Afghan village for more than 80 years and so she was justified in feeling weary. As she reached the only wooden bench in the neighbourhood, she collapsed on it in relief. At the other end of the seat a stranger passed the time of day and she continued her short journey home. Within minutes she was dragged from her home to the village imam. The man from the mosque bypassed the charge and went directly to the punishment for apostasy – talking to the stranger made her apostate and the only sentence open was death. She was made to lay on the ground with a man gripping each of her four limbs. First to be chopped off were her arms and then came the legs. All that remained on the torso was the head which was decapitated with one swift swipe of the machete. This frail widow had lived for 85 years but not once did she expect to end her days as a victim of sharia law. The rumour that Muhammad was a sadist was established long before Maulana emerged. His exploits were barbaric. Cutting off ears and cutting out tongues were commonly conducted by the "prophet." One of his more sadistic practices involved cutting of all the fingers and toes. Once again we uncover the unrestrained brutality of "The Bloody Religion Of Piece."

There are innumerable accounts of savagery. Authority to wage war and commit murder is not just sanctioned in the Quran and Hadith but is enthusiastically encouraged. Journalist Melanie Phillips does not mince her words when she comments, "All that God has made sacred Allah has profaned." Not historically but currently, is a harrowing account of such excoriation,. We predicate that no one has ever heard of Reza Gul, aged 20. This does not surprise us. The young lady was one of the 26,250,000 (Statistic Brain Research Institute) victims of forced marriages in the world each year. She was "married" to Muhammad Khan for a tempestuous time of six years. Throughout that period she was constantly tormented and tortured. In the heart of Taliban territory life can be cheap. Muhammad came home one day and announced to his wife he wanted to marry their 6 year old daughter. If Muhammad the prophet could do it so could he. The thought of the prophet having intercourse with a child is one thing but the prospect of your own daughter having sexual intercourse with her father and your husband, was a horrible thought. Reza was defiant and did all that she could to protect her little girl. Muhammad suddenly left the room but soon returned with a large knife. He began by violently beating Reza, breaking her jaw, nose and fracturing her skull. After pinning her down, he then casually cut off her entire nose! Reza almost bled to death but made it successfully to the nearest medical help with her daughter at her side. It is not surprising that the response to the phrase, "Allah the all Merciful" is greeted with gross contempt. Writer Abdul Ahmed when commenting on such evil, is left with no alternative but to conclude the "The Bloody Religion of Peace" originates in the bowels of hell.

Christians and Jews were classed alongside the unbelievers and their fate was just as repugnant as any unbeliever or idolater. "Fight those who believe not in Allah and the Last Day, nor hold that forbidden by Allah and His Messenger, nor acknowledge the religion of truth, (even if they are) of the People of the Book, until they pay the *jizya* (a tax) with willing submission, and feel themselves subdued" (Sura 9:29). Did you note the double barrelled blast of "subdue" and "submit?" The Muslim mandate from Allah is always centred on subjugation. It is not by coincidence that Islam is another word meaning submission. Islamic propaganda would have people believe that Islam signifies peace but Joseph Wouk lets the cat out of the bag when he annotates, "If Islam means peace why do 97% of the conflicts in the world have Islamic influence?" This does not include the in-fighting between Shia-Sunni Muslim's. Their hatred and hostility has been raging since after Muhammad's death and continues equally as hostile today. Of the ten most evil designated countries in the the world nine are Islamic and the other is North Korean. We are not surprised nor are we impressed.

The word "fight" that was pronounced previously, is the formal Arabic word "*Jihad*." Of all that a Muslim might do this side of the grave, Jihadism is the highest honour or privilege for any adherent of Islam. "Do ye make the giving of drink to pilgrims, or the maintenance of the Sacred Mosque, equal to the pious service of those who believe in Allah and the Last Day, and strive with might and mettle, in Allah's cause (*jihad fi sabil Allah*). They are not comparable in the sight of Allah: and Allah guides not those who do wrong. Those who believe, and suffer exile and contend with force and ferocity in Allah's cause or jihad fi sabil Allah. With their goods and their persons, they have the highest rank in the sight of Allah: they are the people who will achieve salvation" (Sura 9:19-20). As far as the theology of Islam is concerned, jihad fi sabil Allah, rigidly refers to a merciless battling on behalf of Allah and Islam. One debater, Dr. David Wood, summed it up like this, "Muslim's are in a salutary hurry to die – their driven desire for death, is in one sense found in the Quran and in another sense discovered in the Devil.

Before the ink has had time to dry, a newsflash has illustrated precisely what the reality of the above entails. A 12 year old boy walked into a wedding ceremony that was in full flow. It was a typical Turkish occasion with the laughter of many children and their parents happily dancing. No one could possibly know that the uninvited guest was a "suicide bomber" heavily laden with explosives. At just the right time and not one second too soon, the bomb and the boy exploded sending shrapnel through the air to shred the guests into bloody fragments of bone and flesh. Most of the victims were children and the death toll is 51 and rising. Those who committed this callous and cowardly crime were heard to be laughing, while those left alive could only be seen crying. Islamic State, who have superseded ISIS and ISIL, and are now the emerging global caliphate; have gleefully claimed responsibility. The horrific incident sums up the mindset and mentality of savages hell-bent on spilling as much blood as is conceivably possible. This is another episode of the raw and unadulterated Jihad. Who was it that proudly claimed responsibility for this carnage? Yes! It is the "The Bloody Religion of Peace" that has inflicted this agonising anathema.

What on earth could possibly persuade a Muslim, and it is exclusively Islam that carries out these barbarous acts; but what is it exactly that provides the Muslim momentum? Over one billion Muslim's are dyed with the same stain and are compelled to comply with the Quranic constraints. Former Muslim and now Atheist Hirsi Ali, advances that the burning of the Quran would extinguish the fire in Islam. The widely proffered suggestion that there is more than one type of Muslim is resoundly rejected. We are plagued with only one category or curse, and that is the Muslim who holds to a literalist view of the Quran. One of the main reasons why we have this evil phenomenon, is due to the promise of "paradise." We reported elsewhere that it is written in the "Holy Book," that paradise is guaranteed to those who "slay and are slain" (Sura 9:111) for Allah. In the list of 100 of the most eminent Islamic scholars, Fethullah Gulen is found first. His interpretation of this verse concerning "slaying" is confined historically to "battlefield warfare." The fly in the eye problem with that understanding is the literal context. This verse is present day and not past time application only. From the day that Muhammad first held a blood-soaked sword, until this very day, the message has remained unchanged, "slay and are slain."

When we turn the pages of the Bible, and it is to our advantage to do so; we discover it has much to say about peace. When surveying the

King James Bible we expose as many as 429 direct references to peace. Uniquely, we also learn that Jesus is the "Prince of Peace;" The Quran, states Samuel Huntingdon, has a meagre 67 indirect uses of the word peace. It is disappointing, but not surprising, that there are so few pages citing peace by the so-called, "Bloody Religion of Peace?" All that the Quran unearths about peace could be written on the back of a large postage stamp. The absence of peace in the Quran is an embarrassment to those Muslim's advocating peace. The acclaimed author Adnan Oktar believes that the Quran teaches, "love and peace for every human being." Oktar deceitfully informs his readers that "Islam" is simply another word for "peace." This misunderstanding is also a misleading statement that cannot be supported scholarly, from within the Qur'an. Islam has always been translated as "submission" by all moderate academics. Its root word is *"aslama"* which is taken to mean "surrender." The Middle East linguist, Ferros Aboukhadijeh, concedes; "For Islam to mean peace, a great violence would have to be applied to the Arabic word submission."

To have a right regard for scripture is a universal principle but the road to reading it responsibly may be littered with potholes. There are some 6,500 spoken languages in the world today and there are two languages in particular that stand out and for different reasons. The first to adduce, is the most popular language of all, which is Chinese Mandarin, with in excess of 1.4 billion who speak this language. Perhaps, surprisingly for some, is the second language of Arabic. This language is not singled out for its popularity but for what Adam Ahmad refers to as, "The Rule Of Repeal." What makes this language unique is the previously divulged "Law of Abrogation (*naskh*)." In Islam and the Quran it is a language tool used purely as a convenience. There are many Islamic scholars who conveniently circumvent passages in the Qur'an on the back of this suspect and spurious aphorism of abrogation!

An example of this doctrine can be found in the Quran, and it is arguably one of the typically sanguine passages, "I will cast terror into the hearts of those who disbelieve. Therefore strike off their heads and strike off every fingertip of them" (Sura 8:12). It is theologically acceptable for a Muslim to take a text out of context and use it to relegate the significance of what was previously written. In any language it is a cunning act of duplicity. We must keep in tension the fact that not all words or verses in the Quran carry the same weight. Unlike the Bible the Quran is not organised chronologically but rather by the size of the chapters. It was Muhammad himself who acknowledged and justified its use. Classical scholars point out that there is disagreement within Islam over abrogation. As intimated earlier, the Ahmadiyah sect in Pakistan firmly reject this practice since it implies that the Quran is not free from error. Not every Muslim accepts the fringe sect called the Ahmadis. Islamic State uncompromisingly views them as apostates and candidates for death. It suffices to say that there is a tension within Islam and the Quran as to whether god withdrew revelation from Muhammad and the "sacred scripts." Those who voice this view would have to accept that this leaves the door wide open to accusations of inerrancy.

The arguments surrounding the fallibility of Muhammad and the Quran are anything but new. After the extensive dig of The Great Mosque in Yemen, it was declared that precious first century "evidence" had been miraculously unearthed. Quranic manuscripts had been craftily concealed inside the Mosque. As the building was being transformed, much to everyone's surprise; manuscripts fell from the ceiling like raindrops from the sky. Some have happily and readily accepted the account but many others have rejected it outright. What is intriguing, says Abu Bakari, is that Muhammad commissioned a close friend to build The Great Mosque, not in the first century but the sixth century. This controversial episode has been long on speculation but short on evidence. Not surprisingly there have been oceans of conjecture but no watertight facts have surfaced. The intervening prolonged period of five hundred years was axiomatically unforthcoming. We are led to believe today, that the consensus is that no Quranic manuscript, Islamic chronicle, or written catalogue; is to be found anywhere from the first century era. It could be convincingly argued that since Islam was born ca. 570-632, and this is the scholarly position; not even as much as one jot or tittle of Arabic, can purport to originate from the first century.

Expositor Robert Mores emphasises the pivotal point that fallacies run through Islam like the Nile runs through Egypt. There is a dynamic that many Muslims do not understand. We call it "historical precedent." What this means is that the onus of proof rests squarely on the shoulders of those presenting new evidence and not on those who have had their evidence previously ratified. Islam possesses artefacts and historical documents that "suggest" an earlier origin than the seventh century but for many the jury is still out. We need to exercise great concern and caution when an Islamic manuscript is mysteriously engendered and then dated, for it is hugely difficult to apply any accurate dating for ancient scripts. Over the centuries many things have changed but one thing that is constant is the application of the one hundred and more brutal texts tidily tucked away in the Quran. The proof of that is exposed everyday with the countless catalogue of terrorist atrocities.

A child bride, a concept of Muhammad; is just as prevalent a practice now as it ever was before. We have it documented that Muhammad consummated his marriage to Aisha when she was aged between 6 and 9 and he was in his fifties! The Quran calls him a prophet but the stark sobering reality is that the law of the land says he is a paedophile and a multiple-adulterer with an estimated 13 wives! What a huge humiliation that must be for his followers. Most Muslim's recklessly dismiss the lawlessness of Muhammad and simply take them as their moral code. "If Muhammad can do it then so can we." The prophet advocated wife beating, child slavery and honour killing. All these are evident today and it is simply because mindless Muslim's are still blindly emulating Muhammad today.

Another Muhammad – not in Arabia but Afghanistan, who is proudly following in the footsteps of his namesake; is about to be remembered for all the wrong reasons. This middle-aged Muslim man recently "obtained" a 13 year old child-bride who he purchased from her family. On this day in question, one that we will wish never occurred; she was found walking in her village street. Suddenly, as if out of the blue, a man briefly spoke to her as she passed by. She did not reply but continued down the dirt road to her home. Before she had finished washing the dust from her feet, her husband abruptly appeared behind her. He was clearly furious and started to beat her mercilessly. Content that he had battered and bruised her sufficiently, he then chose to tie her hands behind her back. If that was distressing, what happens next is horrifying. Her "husband" took out his knife and cut off the ears of his 13 year old "wife" who he "loved." The screams could be heard at the other end of the village but no-one moved even a muscle.

Why would he, a human being, commit such a monstrous act? Was he suffering from some severe psychiatric illness; perhaps deranged? No. Had his child-bride provoked him, or done anything to make him so enraged? No. What unfolded is that the girl innocently walked by a man who spoke to her. There was no conversation – she did not even lift her head to look at the stranger. It was this inoffensive event that sparked the hard-hearted Muslim man, to explode in anger. The prophet, not Muhammad but Ezekiel, wrote that there is only one cure for such a cruel and callous complaint, "I will give you a new heart and put a new spirit in you; I will remove from you your heart of stone and give you a heart of flesh" (36:26). The heart of the Islamist terrorist problem is the heart.

We will all be appalled by the above account but not all of us will be entirely surprised. Sadly, this and atrocities like it, are common occurrences in Islamic countries, particularly those which practice Sharia Law fully and take the Quran literally. Of course, some Quranic texts are more "elastic" than others but the Hadith provides the necessary licence for latitude. If Muhammad is the quintessential Muslim role model, then Muslim's will be compelled to rightly follow him. After all, amongst other things, Muhammad was a seasoned wife-beater (Sahih Muslim (4:2127) and Muslim's today mirror him and beat their wives regularly and vigorously. Their authority for this is obviously the "sacred texts" like Sahih Bukhari (72:715) and the Quran (4:34; 38:44) which are both in the context of violence against the wife. In fact, the prophet ordered that the wife to be beaten. It was customary for the prophet of Allah to often say...... "beat her or strike her."

The Quran is as diverse as those who turn its pages to read. To Muslim's it is known as the holy book or sacred script. In a literal sense "Recitation" is the meaning of the Arabic word Quran. Muslim's believe that it is a succession of revelations that Muhammad claimed he had from Allah over a period of years. The chapter's or Sura's are not in a literary order or even in any logical scheme. The unravelling of the book is in accordance to weight – the heaviest, or longest chapters appear first and the lightest and shortest, last. The fact that the Quran was still incomplete long after Muhammad died, leaves ample room for speculation. Our understanding of the latter part of the Quran, in the absence of factual evidence, is conjectural. It appears that additional texts were "found" on a variety of material such as bones, stones, leaves and wood. As the colleagues of Muhammad died off, so did the memory of the Quran. Academic Daniel Greenfield deliberated the fundamental flaw with the Quran is the sub-standard construction of the foundation. As with any building, the presence of a solid foundation is imperative if the building is to stand. Unfortunately, the Quran is built on faulty foundations and cannot stand the stiff test of any scholarly scrutiny.

Muslim's argue that the Quran would not be believed by so many today if it was not a true book. That might be so, but it does not wash. We know from the present and the past, that belief does not necessitate truth. There are many millions of deluded Muslims who sincerely believe that if they die a martyr's death they will be catapulted to heaven but this is contemptible. Furthermore, the Quran is not even read by most Muslim's, so their understanding is acquired through an intermediary. In the same way the Roman church fails to read the Bible but turns to a fallible "priest" to disseminate the truth, so does Islam with the Quran. It is anomalous that two opposing religions like Catholicism and Islamism should have something closely in common. Both of their religious books are corrupted and are therefore compromised. In the case of the version of the "Roman Bible," we discover they have added, or included six non-cannonical books, known as the Apocrypha; to the thirty nine originally inspired books. In doing so they have carelessly contradicted the red flag in the book of the Revelation in the Bible, "I testify unto every man that heareth the words of the prophecy of this book, if any man shall unto them, God shall add unto him the plagues which are written in this book: and if any man shall take away from the words of this book of this prophecy, God shall take away his part from the tree of life, and out of the holy city, which are written in this book." Muhammad had the luxury of access to infinite biblical texts when scavenging on Christian camel trains. Unfortunately, he has subsequently disregarded and even disobeyed God's commandments; and all this at great cost to himself.

When we turn to the Quran we find that the Islamic authority, "Basic Principles of the Quran" espouses, "No other book in the world can match the Quran...The astonishing fact about the book of Allah is that it has remained unchanged over the last fourteen hundred years...No variation of text can be found within it. You can check this for yourself by listening to the recitations of Muslims from different parts of the world." It is crucial to keep in tension that the fruit is dependent on the root and not the other way around. The root of the Quran is Muhammad who transmitted this book orally to those around him. It was still being compiled long after his death. Throughout the last fourteen centuries it has been transmitted from man to man. Since so many Quranic scholars dispute the differences and contest the contradictions, there is no merit here in undoing all the wrong they have done. It is more than sufficient to say that the four principal Imams, who founded the Hanafi, Maliki, Shafi'i and Hanbali schools of Islamic Jurisprudence are all in disagreement about "the perfect book" - the Quran.

Abu Sayyaf, a terrorist turned teacher, suggests a theoretical synopsis concerning the Quran and the author. A forensic scientist does not work with speculation but exclusively with evidence. If we were to examine the Quran we should also avoid anything speculative and assay the evidence of the author and his book. Should we turn the clock back 1400 years, Muslim's would expect to find the "finger prints" of Allah and his messenger. Needless to say that ascertaining both these would be important and expedient, or as the French say, *tout de suite*. Since our position denies the existence of Allah, accept in the form a figment of man's imagination; we can safely rule out his prints being present. Should we accept that the origin of the Quran was born in a cave named Hira, it would be reasonable to expect some semblance of evidence. Unfortunately, this hypothesis is replete with difficulty. If we agree that the angel Gabriel conveyed the Quran to Muhammad then we have to believe the Quran was inspired – God given. Here again we have to submit that none of the "evidence" supports the view that Muhammad was the recipient of Allah's words (godly). The alternative view, which is exceedingly more convincing; is that Muhammad concocted the Quran after his numerous experiences and exchanges with the Jewish and Christian caravans that traversed the far-flung Arabia desert.

We wonder when will European government's act instead of react? Europe is lurching dangerously near the edge of a bottomless pit and the number one concern seems to be the dubious distraction of Climate Change! The West is in the throes of acute cognitive dissonance over Islam and we are worried about the CO_2 emissions from church candles. We have failed to acknowledge that Islamic State (IS) have picked up their book and have declared war on us but astonishingly, and the whole of Europe ought to be astounded; we have not declared war on IS. Can you imagine a burglar saying, "I'm going to rob your house tonight," and you do absolutely nothing. In fact, you go as far as to leave the key in the door! This is the ridiculous role acted out on the western stage between the European Union and the Islamic State. It is utterly incomprehensible but this is the farcical scenario that is eked out by almost every country.

Refreshingly and encouragingly, unlike its neighbours, Hungary is divided by only the River Danube. The ten million population are all united in there rejection of rabid Islam. Hungary is landlocked and surrounded by countries who physically fear Islam but the Prime Minister, Victor Orban, is the only vocal leader to speak up in the face of overwhelming opposition. The PM articulated to European leaders that the problem was one of "mathematics." "The more migrants we accept – the more terrorism we expect." Orban closed with this statement, "Islam is terrorising the West not because it can but because it is allowed." His speech proved productive with the evidence of fresh fruit. Boldly and bravely, Slovakia's Andrej Kiska, Beata Maria Szydlo, the Polish Prime Minister and Marine Le Pen of France all voiced close co-operation in resisting the Islamisation of what is commonly called "Eurabia." Europe has opened its doors to the migrants and refugees and in gratitude the migrants and refugees have slammed the door in Europe's face.

Thank God there are leaders and countries that still stand on the rock of democracy which is at variance with the toxic ideology of the Quran and Islam. We ought not to be surprised to discover that the richest country in the world happens to be one of the most pernicious. Amnesty International lists Saudi Arabia as one of the top three for despicable acts of public execution. The latest figures for 2016 is a total 154 open-air public executions. Some of these are impromptu and spontaneous roadside murders. Saudi Arabia keeps good company in that it rubs shoulders with China, Iran and North Korea; all of which are the main rogue states. It is significant that when an execution takes place a copy of the Quran is inevitably present as if to give some perverse notion that the murder is authorised. As this book goes to print a man is sitting in a Saudi cell awaiting execution. His crime? He says he does not believe in anything. He is one of the many millions who are known as atheist's. It appears for Islam and the Muslim, the possession of an intellect is not a prerequisite for finding faith or choosing a religion such as theirs. Being brainless and unable to even contemplate a religion is apparently unimportant. In any event this poor man remains sitting in his cell waiting to see the razor-sharp sword that will promptly remove his head. His basis for not accepting Islam and the Quran is elementary – he unsurprisingly doesn't believe it. Whenever there is an exchange between the Quran and the Bible, a Muslim and a Christian; the Muslim will vehemently besmirch the Bible in order to justify his Quran. But this is an argument based on error and not truth. A Christian believes the Bible not because the Quran is false but because the Bible is true. This is why Saudi Arabia needs the Bible more than its black gold.

We have heard the Quran was from Allah because Muhammad said and we know Muhammad spoke for Allah because the Quran says. The Quran has much to say about many things so we should not be surprised to find that it has something to say about us. The Quran and Muhammad use many words but pitifully say very little. We can agree that the most important aspect raised in their religious book is arguably, the matter of Salvation. In the essay by Tom McMahon he raises the issue that there are between 4200 – 4500 religions in the world. All of them ridiculously confess that their religion is true. The crux of McMahon work is that it is not possible to find Christianity anywhere in the lengthy list of worldwide religions. The reason for this is that all of them, with the exception of

Christianity, have a core component called "faith" missing. Like Pharaoh they were all heard to say, "I do not know the Lord." World religions have all been man-made which tells us they are in fact home-grown cults. We concur with Christine Williams definition of a cult; "A cult is a religious system headed by an individual who is perceived as a venerated person." The most relevant cult is of course Islam, which true to form heralds a man as its leader. Muhammad's man-made cult was apparently hatched in a cave and his first "converts" or followers, were his reticent relatives. From this trickle a tsunami of terror has increasingly flooded the landscape of the world. History reveals that many cult leaders have been nothing more than evil despots and Muhammad has proved to be the worst of the worse; the ultimate in callous and cruel cult leaders. It comes as little consolation that cults routinely come and go and we have every reason to believe that Islam will eventually be confined to the history books.

It is widely known that the Christian lives by faith and that the Muslim lives by fear. The dynamic of faith in Christ is what separates Christianity from all the other specious belief systems that exist today. For a Muslim reality is found in the most sobering of dogmas, which is their doctrine of salvation by works (Sura 11; 7:8,9). Each and every Muslim has to climb the inescapable ladder of salvation with great trepidation and through their own works and by their own efforts. Islam erroneously teaches and Muslim's irrationally believe that if they live a "good life" – if they do more good than bad, they will be miraculously translated from earth to heaven. It all sounds rather simple but there is a clause. Every Muslim has a symbolic "weighing scale" which will reveal at death all that they have done in life. Eternity hangs in the balance. The theory is that Allah controls the scales and determines who is dispatched to hell and who is delivered to heaven. It all hinges on the all-important scales and whether a Muslim is left found wanting. The prospect of gaining any ground or finding any favour, is for the Muslim; wholly dependent upon a mythical Allah.

There is one more salient point to ponder and that is the "guaranteed" means of Muslim salvation. This procedure has no hidden strings attached and there is no small print to read. Islamic literature like the Quran and Hadith, which speak loudly about the Jihadist and the martyr; is uncompromisingly emphatic. The martyr is commonly referred to as *Shahid* or *Shaheed* in Arabic. Once again there is some disagreement about terminology. We need to be crystal clear that suicide, in itself, is against Islamic indoctrination. However, martyrdom is not afforded that same luxury. The Quran determines, "And there is the type of man who gives his life to earn the pleasure of Allah…" This would not be in the Quran if it were not permissible (Quran 2:207). The next verse is one of the more abhorrent, "And do not kill anyone which Allah has forbidden, except for a just causation." A just or unjust cause are equally reprehensible. This is the primary coveted text amongst Islamic martyrs, to not only justify their own death, but also that of bystanders who might also be Muslim's. When all is said and done, the end justifies the means; with the goal being to defeat every kaffir, to impose Sharia Law and to establish a world-wide Caliphate (Quran 17:3). This is the global Islamic plan and the purpose of both denominations within Islam; Sunni and Shia.

The route to heaven for the Muslim is a perilous one. It is accepted that those who kill the infidel and are killed receive a promise of bliss in the eternal realm. It is often incorrectly reported that this is a black and white Quranic doctrine; it is an Islamic fact. We can confirm that Muhammad and the Hadith have references concerning *virgins* and *boys* as a heavenly reward. We find relevant details in Suna 4 and chapter 21. The salutation "suicide bomber" poses a petulant problem. The conclusion and consensus, is that it is specifically a western expression and is therefore rejected as a non-Islamic term. Allah is telling Muslim's if you can murder as many non-Muslims (infidels) as possible and die in the process, I will make the hope of heaven a reality. What is more obnoxious than this is that there are up to a billion Muslims who have swallowed such a preposterous proposal. A god that orders and ordains his followers to kill and be killed is a maleficent monster.

It is accepted that William Shakespeare wrote a total of ten tragedies or plays. Each one had something in common. They all included a character that met a tragedy or experienced a misfortune. The series of tragedies beg the question what might be the greatest tragedy of all. This matter is both speculative and subjective. Nevertheless, the all time titanic tragedy to ever smite humanity, is without question Muhammad and his Muhammadan's. Unfortunately, Muhammad is not just the conductor of licentiousness but he is also the orchestrator of lies. We know from Scripture that the devil lies, in fact, he is known as the "Father of Lies." The devil and Muhammad would appear to be in good company. Writing in his latest work John Ankerberg comments, "Muhammad qualifies as the greatest liar for denying the divinity of Christ." He is convinced that Islam's prophet was an inveterate liar. The denial of The Christ comes at a colossal cost and the price is one that mankind cannot afford to pay. The New Testament words of Matthew 10:33 make the aftermath of such an error perfectly plain, "...Whoever disowns me (Jesus) before others, I will disown before my Father in heaven."

We are apprised by Jihad Watch, "The ultimate deception of all time is the fact that over one billion Muslims have been betrayed." Muhammad is the plank which all of his followers are forced to walk. He is humanly responsible for leading men, women and children to the brink of the abyss. The devil has made "paradise" an attractive proposition with endless physical promises to satisfy the flesh. Muslims have naively bought into the hope of heaven not realising it will never be manifested. The Christian knows that Jesus proclaims in John 14:6, "... No one comes to the Father except through Me." Disastrously, the devil has misled Muslim's into believing they can foolishly find their own way to heaven. Muhammad is well versed in deception and highly schooled in the art of lying, and both of these traits are at the expense of countless souls sinking deeper in to darkness. There are few vices as accursed as a bold faced lie. The philosophical patriarch, Friedrich Nietzsche, sorely stated, "I am upset that you lied to me but I am more upset because now I can no longer believe you," Today, over 22% of the population have believed Muhammad, the mastermind of lies.

Manchester on Monday evenings will never be the same. A man stood alone murmuring under his breath a verse he had repeated day and night; *"And kill them wherever you find them, and turn them out from where they turned you out. And Al-Fitnah (disbelief) is worse than killing...but if they desist, then lo! Allah is forgiving and merciful. And fight them until there is no more Fitnah (disbelief) and worship is for Allah alone"* (Quran 2:191-2). This is merely one of a hundred and one poisonous passages in the Islamic "holy book" that calls for the murder of anyone and everyone that is not a Muslim. The suicide bomber that blew himself up and killed or injured so many innocent people, had this verse in his heart as the bomb detonated. He committed this massacre in the name of god (Allah), which reveals to us a great deal about the abhorrent nature of Allah. The bomber was particularly ruthless packing his explosive device full of nuts and bolts for maximum impact and optimum casualties. The force of those pieces of metal was so great it dismembered victims. It is well known that the press are quick to get things wrong and slow to get them right. One journalist, Katty Kay, will be wishing today that the ground swallows her up. After the London bombings, and during a moment of madness, she made this broadcast, "I suppose we are just going to have to get used it." Really? No! Would she say the same thing about the migrant robberies and rapes, the knife and acid attacks? Would Kay say the same thing about child brides, honour killings that occur day in and day out? What about the presence of sharia law and sharia patrols in Muslim ghettoes, that the press, police and parliament deceitfully deny? Get used to it!

The reason this Muslim murderer carried out such a cold-blooded and catastrophic crime, is because at some point he had an intellectual conversion. We have said it before and we say it again; Muslim's of all ages, have been indoctrinated in the mosques by the mullah's. Do not forget that Islam is anything but religious – that is simply a guise or ruse. We would call Islam a political ideology that is coated with icing sugar. A development that compounds the Islamic ideological position is that sales of Mein Kampf have escalated with nine out ten customers being Islamic. Of all the prominent component parts of Islam there is one that is overlooked. Allah and the Quran are heartless and therefore loveless. A Muslim is born with a stone hard heart and he will die with the same heart if it is not changed. The cowardly mass murderer, Salman Abedi, had that same inherent heart. Fox News presenter Sean Hannity summarises, "When this savage opened his eyes after the explosion; it was not in the warmth of paradise but to his horror, it was in the heat of hell."

This Muhammad believed it was possible to avoid hell. This is not an original or authentic doctrine. In essence all this amounts to is just another misguided Muhammadan spin. We will not be surprised if we discern that the source of this deluded dogma is buried in the Quran (19:70, 4:95). This leaves one believing the possible avoidance of hell as a reality. The Pope and the Roman church have adopted the same duplicitous diatribe. Every Quran (Sura 69, 84:7) instructs the Muslim to believe that they will go to hell for their sins but after paying a "fine" they are released to enter paradise. (There is no mention which currency will be acceptable!). Nevertheless, their good news is that the only cast iron guarantee of being propelled to paradise is through Jihad (Quran 3:169, 9:39). The logic behind this ultimatum is twisted. If a Muslim kills a kaffir in battle, the kaffir takes the Muslim's place in hell. These words are empty and worthless. They amount to another one of those monumental misleading myths procreated by a Islam.

It is possible to prove that Muslim's are heartless. Since there is no conjecture between the unholy trinity of Allah, Muhammad and the Quran; they must be in total agreement. In Idaho there is a lovely little girl called Lacy. She is just five and lives alone with her mum. One day when she was playing in the yard; three Muslim youths grabbed her and carried her in to a nearby laundry room. For the next 30 minutes this gentle child endured the sort of suffering that no animal should. The three Muslim's savagely raped her, orally, vaginally and anally. For good measure and to remind her of the so-called supremacy of Muslim's over infidel's, all three urinated in her mouth and over her face. We do not think Lacy will ever forget the day that Allah came to visit. Do you?

Most Islamic scholars believe that Muslim's can use rape as terror (*Kiribati*). We also find conveniently in Quran 2:282, "The testimony of a woman is half that of a man." Syria's chief Mufti, Sheikh Abe al-Rahman Ali al-Dala gives a green light to Muslim's raping the enemy (infidel's). It is the height of hypocrisy to hear clinical cleric's cold-heartedly state, "Any sexual misdemeanour's between Muslim's requires the woman to present 4 male witnesses. The rape of a non-Muslim by a Muslim is treated so ambivalently it amounts to indifference (Quran 4:24). This episode is an example of the injustice and the grave disparity that we find folded in the pages of the Quran. And Lacy? The lilly-livered Judge succumbed to fear – fear of stepping on someone's politically correct toes and the horror of being called an Islamophobic, racist and bigot. The Muslim youth's did what they do well and escaped free. And Lacy? Well, she and her mum left in a torrent of tears.

It is impossible to understand Jihad terrorists without the Quran. If you want to know why Muslim's commit multiple murders it is essential to have in your hand the Quran, or Islamic "holy book." The Jihadist will boastfully quote (misquote) the Quran and say that they are pursuing the "pure way." There are others such as the Council on American Islamic Relations (C.A.I.R.) would argue the Jihadis' are using and even abusing the Quran, for self-fulfilling purposes. In 2007 David Plotz surveyed the Bible but he made a fundamental mistake. He wrote what he thought and felt and produced a subjective outcome. Many readers of the Quran fall in to the same hole as Plotz and provide a purely introspective account. Possession of a Quran is the cure for this complaint.

What Barak Obama thinks or what Pope Francis thinks, is immaterial, if it is outside of the Quran. In Islamic theology the Quran is essentially an Arabic Quran. This is supported by Robert Spencer who informs us, "The blizzard of other language translations (non-Arabic) do not strictly adhere to the Quran." There are a multitude of hardline Muslim scholars who religiously maintain that unless the Quran is translated in Arabic, it should be left on the shelf. What is quite extraordinary is the requirement for adherents to read the Quran in Arabic, when the vast majority of Muslim's cannot read a word of Arabic. Many Muslim's turn to Abdullah Ysuf Ali and Mohammad Marmaduke Pickthall as two of the most popular and eloquent translators in circulation today. Those who hurl words around such as racist, bigot and Islamophobe are demonstrating their ignorance of the Quran. It is essential to keep in tension that as every coin has two sides so does the Quran, Not every Quranic expositor is in agreement. For instance the Quran Sunnath Society under Jamithabeevi is much more progressive and liberal in its interpretation, The stability of the Quran is dependent not on the text but on the handler. All liquids are known as being unstable but what is not known so is the Quran is equally unstable. What is phenomenal is the reverberation by Nonie Darwish, "Incredibly, Muhammad himself was filled full of uncertainty about Islam and the Quran. It is ironic that a false prophet should be prophesying so incitefully about future events.

"He is no fool who gives what he cannot keep, to gain what he cannot lose."

– James Elliot

Chapter Four

Islam

"The Christian martyr says; "I will die for what I believe."
The Muslim martyr says; "You will die for what I believe."

-T. E. Lawrence

There have been more books written on Islam in the last twenty five years than the last two hundred and twenty five. All of these works have tended to direct attention to specific subjects such as Islam and War and The Politics of Islam. However, there has been one book by Robert Spencer that has gone the extra mile by adopting a comprehensive approach. "Islam Unveiled," spills the beans and exposes with clarity the ingrained violent nature of this belief system. It is quite extraordinary that proponents of Islam would have us believe that Islam means peace. What makes the comment so ridiculous is that all of the campaigns and conquests waged by Islam have been achieved not by peace but by force. We should not be surprised to discover that Islam actually translates as "submission," and of course, submit to Allah. This account will no doubt cause the likes of President's Clinton, Bush and Obama to choke on their words that Islam means peace. Apologist's for Islam are quick to point out that the Bible is equally abhorrent but there is a blatant difference that is conveniently overlooked. The god of the Quran sanctions endless acts of violence and the God of the Bible does not advocate any.

For over 1,400 years Islam has had its sword drawn from the scabbard in order to subjugate and denigrate every civilisation that has had the misfortune to be in its path. It seems more people are asking questions about Islam this year than any other year. A decisive description of Islam that addresses the primary question being asked, is proposed by the scholar Dr. Bill Warner, "Islam is a cultural, religious and political system." It is the latter which is proving to be so problematic and which is making non-Muslims most apprehensive. The Islamic political system is wrapped up in the *Quran* (words of Allah), the *Hadith* (the traditions of Muhammad) and the *Sira* (the biography of Muhammad). This is not the only trilogy in the Islamic text and it does not appear by coincidence. We will see elsewhere that there are adumbrations of Christianity to be found folded in the pages of certain texts. *Najaran* was an ancient Christian City situated over 1,000 miles south of Medina. Muhammad is known to have been a perennial visitor trading in what we colloquially call camel's; "Ships of the Desert." This location was a significant and strategic commercial centre with Christian caravan's of camel's frequently flowing through. It is inevitable, writes Dr. John Morrow, the Arabic academic, "Muhammad would have imbibed core Christian tenets at this time and that is why shadows of Christianity are manifested in Quranic doctrine and Islamic literature" What we can declare historically and with absolute confidence is that Christianity is the religion of peace and Islam is certainly not.

The media repeatedly spoon feeds society with lavish lumps of misinformation and nowhere is that more prevalent than with the matter of prickly Islam. We are routinely duped in to believing the deceitful statement, "Islam is a religion of Peace." Many Muslim's will tell you one thing to your face and say something else behind your back. This conniving behaviour is not the exception but the rule. A classical example of this is Barak Hussein Obama, a former President of the United States, who is heard incessantly saying; "Islam means peace." His private view is some what different to his public opinion, where he confusingly concedes; "Islam means submission." Although he has professed Christianity; he does not lead us to believe he has met Christ." The Bangladesh writer Muhammad Sharon believes, "Born a Muslim and die a Muslim." Barak's dualism or syncretism, may mislead many but it receives a thumbs down from the discerning. Since "Hussein" shares a bed with the Muslim Brotherhood and the Council for American Islamic Relations (CAIR), both rancorous terrorist fronts; this makes the Ex-President complicit, or as La Croix reported, "Obama is an adulterous slut." To pour petrol on Obama's simmering situation, we find that he has diverted American money towards two other godless groups of terrorism; Hamas (Islamic resistance) and *Hezbollah* (The Party of god). Obama is stiff-necked and obstinately defiant that Islam is a religion of peace. Robert Spencer is equally uncompromising when he elucidates, "The President's four closest allies were Islamic and his four greatest enemies were also Islamic." The strategist, David Horowitz, an accomplished author, sets the record straight by confirming what is widely agreed; "Obama has been justifiably referred to as the worst President in history who spent more time talking about peace than he did practising it."

Ironically, at precisely the same moment and just as Obama was commenting on Islam and peace, Gaucherie Bobokulova was committing a crime that would horrify the world. The 38 year old nanny had been working in northern Moscow for several years and was trusted with the care of 4 year old, Anastasia. On this day lives would be turned upside down and hearts broken into pieces. Anastasia's nanny took the largest knife out of the kitchen; the one she used for cutting meat from the market and promptly went into the bedroom of Anastasia. The nanny then proceeded to sit on the child and to wrench her hair and head back. With the butcher's knife held for cutting, Bobokulova sliced through the tender neck of the child until the head was severed. The cot of the infant soon became a blood-bath and as the "executioner" looked down at the devastating scene the woman had committed, she smiled sardonically at her debased "handy work."

Throughout the ordeal a Quranic verse was echoing in her head, "I will cast terror in to the hearts of those who disbelieved. Therefore strike off their heads" (Quran 8:12). To everyone's utter abhorrence the Burkha-clad Bobokulova went out on to the street to parade up and down brandishing the swinging head and screaming, *"Allahu Akbah"* (god is greater). When asked by the authorities why she carried out such a gruesome killing of a poor defenceless little girl, her stern reply was, "Allah told me I must do it."

This is raw Islam – crude and cruel. Western leaders like Merkel and May are intoxicated with Islam and are radically wrong in their understanding and with their ministry of misinformation. There is absolutely no peace whatsoever in Islam. The demonic deed carried out on dear Anastasia, is indubitably classical Islam, "The Bloody Religion of Peace." Such atrocious acts only serve to reinforce Islam's satanic stamp of approval.

Having read the barbaric account above, it is inconceivable that any sane person would wish to be loosely connected to, or, even vaguely associated with; such an evil entity as Islam. Surprisingly, it is allegedly Islam that is the "religion" that proffers most in the world. As unbelievable as it seems, Islam has in the region of a billion (United Nations) followers which is comparable with Roman Catholicism (La Santa Sede) and its members. The fact that Islam is a politico-religious movement, infers that it has two edges to its sword, one political and the other religious. This suggests that its capability to cut geographically deeper and wider is further increased. We know that Islamic doctrine is governed by the *Quran*, *Hadith* and *Sunna*. The so-called "Holy Book" (Quran) is said to be the very words of Allah as given to his last prophet Muhammad. As Muhammad was illiterate this is highly questionable and will be addressed abroad. When we turn to the Hadith we are informed that they are the sayings of Muhammad, while the Sunna is a biographical account of the prophets life. Whether researching, reading or reporting, all three texts must be carefully considered if an informed opinion is to be achieved. There is one thing which we can be certain and that is what we see is not always what we get. A cursory reading of any Islamic literature, will soon make perfectly plain that beneath its innocuous religious veneer; lies a sinister contrivance. It is universally accepted that for a fire to burn it is essential to have fuel. Islam is no different. What makes Islam burn; the fuel that keeps the fire ablaze is hatred. Muslim's have a pathological hatred for all non-Muslim's and an overwhelming perverse love of death.

The Pope has surprisingly suggested that the solution to the Islamic intrusion and the current flood of immigrants across Europe, is an open door policy that makes them all welcome. This is merely another inscrutable suggestion that once again reveals an ignorance and a naivety of the Islamic *parti pris*. Most conscientious parents would try to ensure their children went to bed at a reasonable time and so Mark was not surprised when his father said at 9.30 pm, it was time for him to go to bed. The son said good night to his family and went up to his room. At about 10.30 pm he was disturbed from his sleep by a hand over his mouth and a knife on his neck. An Afghan "refugee," who had been warmly welcomed by the family was now a fox in the hen house. The family did as the Pope had said and opened their home to this man. Over the next 30 minutes, the 20 year old man repeatedly raped and sodomised the 10 year old boy. This vile intruder who attacked the child, knew every letter of the following Islamic text, "And they will be given to drink a cup whose mixture is of ginger, a fountain within paradise named Salsabeel. There will circulate among them young boys made eternal. When you see them, you would think them scattered pearls. And when you look there, you will see pleasure and great dominion" (Quran 76:17-20). When the so-called refugee had finished his despicable deed and before he left, he bribed Mark with some "hush money." It is significant that he was an Afghan because the men are notoriously known for preferring little boys to grown women. The words from the Bible, are not circumstantial but consequential, "Thou lovest evil more than good" (Psalm 52:3). The debased villain will not only pay for his crime in this life but he is highly likely to pay in the life to come.

When Rome heard this sickening story the Vatican remained deafeningly silent. "Open your homes and open your doors," said the Pope. Francis welcomes Islamic State Sheiks as "brothers" and kisses the feet of *"Al-Shabaab,"* the Somali-based Muslim terrorists. Is this really true? Yes, really! The Pope's proposition of an open door policy for refugees is a foolish fantasy! Islam is many things but it is not a religion of peace. It is common knowledge that Islamic literature states there are 72 virgins waiting in "paradise" for every Muslim martyr to spend his endless days copulating with. We would be short changed if we did not pause to draw attention to this issue of "virgins." Firstly, the application is strictly for Muslim "martyrs" who murderously slaughter the innocent. A representation of "martyrdom" is the recent suicide bomber who was detonated by remote control in a boisterous Baghdad market. The explosion shredded and killed more than 51 souls, leaving their flesh hanging from trees and their vivid red blood splattered on the white-washed walls. Of course, the Islamic interpretation of "martyr" is so defaced that its true identity is unrecognisable. Islam has corrupted the meaning of the word in such away that it is nothing more than a narcissistic entity. Secondly, this is not as many wrongly believe, a Quranic promise, but an innuendo or debatable term tucked inside the Hadith. Influential imam Sheikh Ysuf Estes, a leading authority; is unequivocal when adducing the source of "virgins" as being buried in the Hadith.

Islamic jurisprudence consistently states that Allah affirmed, not only pretty pristine virgins but also innocent infant boys; would all be waiting in heaven to wet their perverse sexual appetites. This obnoxious irreligious concept would never be found in a holy book; for the moment it was found, the book would cease to be holy. The following words pour light on the subject in question, "And there will go around boy servants of theirs, to serve them as if they were scattered pearls" (Quran 52:24). Pearls, in Islamic rhetoric, are consistently expounded as "boys." The noted American presenter, Joe Cortina, confidently claims that two of the biggest lies in the world have there roots bedded in Islam. "Firstly, it is increasingly popular among the Muslim occupiers of "Gaza" and the "West Bank" to deny the holocaust and the extermination of six million Jews and others, but popularity is not the correct benchmark for establishing truth. Adolf Hitler was very popular but there was not a grain of truth in his baneful body. Secondly, the other outrageous lie uttered by Islam is the repeated promise in the stipulation of coveting 72 virgin's in a so-called paradise. This notion is intimated in the Islamic Holy Book (Quran 16:22, 78:33) but does not specify 72. We have to turn to the Hadith (2687) where it unambiguously alludes to the figure 72. Cortina continues, "If Muslim martyr's believed the truth rather than a lie, there would be no plague of Muslim martyrs!"

There are more people today than there were yesterday, who are convinced that Islam and peace are poles apart and bear no resemblance whatsoever. What else is changing gear, is that the number of men and women who are questioning the legitimacy of Islam, is accelerating. The fall out from Islamic barbarism and butchery has not helped their aggressive agenda to form a global caliphate. Only recently they seized a mother and her four young children and burned them like you would logs on the fire. The screams were horrifying. When the despicable foul feat was carried out; all that remained was five piles of ashes. If you are wondering what scurrilous crime did they possibly commit; they simply wanted to escape the Islamic State. At long last, people are using their eyes to see and their ears to hear and the net result is that they are not warming to towards the opprobrious revilement. Islamic State have been described by *Aadesh Mishra*, as "the epitome of evil" and are nothing more than a group of ruthless reprobates. It is no secret that Islam has an insatiable appetite for blood, so it is not by coincidence, or providence, that Islam is auspiciously renamed, "The Bloody Religion of Peace."

Customarily, most religions have a community of believers dedicated to worship of the Divine. Adherents go around feeding the hungry and clothing the poor. Faiths or beliefs, generally have at least one thing in common and that is to live peaceably and amicably amongst each other. This is how civilised people behave but unfortunately since Islam is uncivilised, it it is impossible for them to integrate or assimilate. They simply do not have the tools or skills in which to operate as a corroborated member of the human race. Muslim's are said to be so unconscionable that the two sects of Islam, *Shiite* (Arabic "faction" with leaders via descendants) and *Sunni* (Arabic "tradition" after Muhammad's successors) are analogous enemies that are hell bent on a bitter campaign to kill each other. Any suggestion that Islam is peaceful is lost in the pages of its "manual for war." The Quran must be read but be prepared for a rough ride. There are numerous imperatives in its pages but to love your neighbour as yourself, is an intractable alien concept. Much is mentioned about the lust of the flesh but any reference to sacrificial love is as rare as the crown jewels.

It will be invaluable at this juncture if we look at some of the myths and tales told about Islam. Islamic propaganda has produced many creases in our reasoning, so it is imperative that we take hold of the truth and iron out those folds. One of the most familiar misconceptions is that Islam means "peace." It should be noted that more myths have originated within the Muslim academic community than all the other graduate institutions put together. Brigitte Gabriel proposes if Islam means peace then why have 270,000,000 men, women and children been annihilated in the name of Allah? Islam and peace are incompatible terms, they are extraneous. Arabic apologist's tend to make the same juvenile mistake by stating the root word of Islam is *"al-Salaam"* which in Arabic means "peace." Take an Arab word – anyone you wish? What you consistently find is that there is one root to one word. This is an elementary principle of Arabic language. The root word for Islam is *"al-silm,"* which means "surrender" or "submission." There is a unison amongst conservative scholars, like Dr Daniel Pipes, who agrees with the above rendering. This leaves us with another crease to iron. The Qur'an tells Muslim's that they have to be in submission to Allah but the sting in the tail is, that the infidel, or unbeliever, must also be in submission whether he likes it or not. Those who have "declined" the closed "invitation" have never lived long enough to reconsider the consequences.

The raw reality of Islam is that it is brutal and savage. Of course, the heart of someone in the Islamic State is physically no different to any one else. We know from the prophet Jeremiah (36-26), "...the heart is deceitful and above all things desperately wicked..." and contrary to what Islam says, this vital verse applies to them. There are some whose heart has such a propensity for wickedness that it is illimitable. An exemplification of this is retold by Newsman Norman Byrd. Nine teenagers were accused of "fraternising" with the enemy (passing the time of day). This concerns the Muslim Islamic State and the Muslim Free Syrian Army. The court was assembled and dismissed in the same breath. Those charged were found guilty but did not attend the Sharia Court and had no idea of the verdict. As each of the boys was chained to an upright metal pole they soon discovered the sentence was going to be death. Suddenly, there was the sound of a small petrol engine starting up and everyone's eyes became fixated. The crowd was as usual large, and excitable. The IS man walked up and down smiling in front of the teenage boys as he revved the petrol powered chain-saw. He then stepped forward and dismembered each one – he cut them in half with the chain saw. The scene resembled a battlefield with blood, bone and body parts littering the roadside. As the young men screamed in agony, on the other side of the road the crowd cheered and waved their symbolic black IS flags. "The Bloody Religion of Peace" was once again duly satiated.

Parallel to this truculent fear-filled execution, there was a sanctimonious political meeting being held simultaneously in the U.K. by the Prime Minister. Theresa May proceeded to tell the public, "I am immensely proud of the contribution that Muslims and Islam have contributed to the U.K. Not surprisingly, she never actually elaborated on the "contribution". Even though her statement was meant to be sober and serious, many could be heard contemptuously laughing loudly. She spoke about pie-in-the-sky areas of British Society that had benefited incredibly from the presence of pious and moral Muslims. But May has made a mistake and is guilty of being fallacious. Her view of "contribution" is seriously detached from reality. The kinds of contribution that Islam has made to the U.K. is shameful and scandalous. Islam has caused the prison population to bulge by a staggering 15% (Prison Reform Trust) and each prisoner costs the tax payer a whopping £65k (PRT) a year. Prisons are now being segregated because Islam are converting more inside than outside prison. The writer Danny Shaw kindly informs us that 30% (PRT) of Muslim prisoners are not British but Somali and Pakistani. Of course, there is more; forced marriages, female genitalia mutilation and honour killings, are not rare but a common occurrence. The shameful rape culture and sexual assaults that are mysteriously flying under the radar, are overlooked by the cowardly police, who spinelessly fear being labelled Islamophobe. We have all this contention and commotion, which is all tangible, but we have yet to address the proliferation of home-grown terrorism. The P.M. Has missed the mark by a mile. All Mrs. May has achieved is to placate the "Islamic Supremacists" who will not be content until they have her head severed. Great Britain once had a P.M. who was known as the "Iron Lady" but unfortunately today we have been landed with Prime Minister who is perched on the proverbial fence and is more flocculent than she is forthright.

The *Daesh*, which is an abbreviation for Islamic State, have as their two arms, Shariah and Jihad. These words, contrary to what we are told; are not separate but closely connected. Sharia and jihad are like a hand and glove. To provide a degree of respectability, some would try to keep Islam apart from Jihad. However, trying to separate one from the other is like attempting to remove the ring from a church bell. The *Yazidis* (Kurdish) are a close-knit peaceful protestant group that have roamed Iraq for countless centuries. They are the bitter enemy of IS by virtue of the fact they are not Islamic but a diminutive religious minority. Islam's hatred for the Yazidis burns hotter than any furnace fire. IS possesses an unremitting revulsion for these people that is palpable. The prolonged persecution of the Yazidis is nothing less than unprecedented. No one is spared – not even the newly born.

A fierce gun battle began between the Yazidis and IS grew as they tried to flee. The screaming of the children pierced the Sinjar mountain air. When the Yazdis began to run out of ammunition, the women, children and some men, attempted to make a break for the hills. Many of them were shot and killed. As the Yazidis guns fell silent the IS ran amongst them shooting them in the head and stabbing them in the heart. The account of this sadistic slaughter was verified by the Yazidi Human Rights Organisation. Naturally, the women and children were slower running to the hills and so they were picked off easily – one after another they fell on their face after being shot in the back of the head. Those who could not outrun IS were captured and kept for the night. The girls and women were gathered together to be used and abused as sex slaves. IS singled out the girls and women they wanted but some dissented to co-operate. Their fate would be repulsive. The Daesh rounded up those who refused to be sex slaves. They then took some primitive farming tools such as sickles and scythes and one by one they decapitated each girl and woman. This macabre and murderous "triumph" for "The Bloody Religion of Peace," is one of thousands.

If we had only one problem with Islamic doctrine then that would be one too many. Precariously, Islam is like a bed of nails for no matter which way you turn you are faced with excruciating pain. The average Muslim, or the Quran believing Islamist, accepts that Islam is the superlative answer. "Not so," says Alan Winters. He convincingly elucidates; why Islam are not the solution to the problems of life. "In the Quran there are exhortations to kill non-believers and be killed. That imperative stretches to lapsed or apostate Muslims." This distinction is comprehensive and leaves no room for loop-holes. Even sitting on the Quran fence is ruled out. It would be wrong to regard the latter as "Good Muslims" because there is no such creature. What differentiates the two groups, is their activity or passivity. It is the state of the heart that is peremptory. We concede that God knows best when he reminds us that the natural heart is as hard as stone, when it ought to be as soft as flesh.

Theologian, Dr. Aiden Tozer, preached for almost half a century that there were only two kinds of people inhabiting the earth. He did not mean black or white or even rich and poor. He maintained the unpopular truth that a man was either a child of the devil or a child of God. It is perfectly plain that the driving force in the Islamist is a hatred that emanates with the devil. It would be absurd to suggest that what propels Islam is an abiding love, for such a quality is an alien concept to the Jihadist. Everyone that has ever met their demise at the hands of malignant Islam would testify that the Muslim hatred was devilish. A case in point is the nation of Israel and the Jews. Apologists argue that the so-called occupation of Palestine is what really fans the flames of hatred that burns in a Muslim heart against the Jewish nation. We need not procrastinate here but it is sufficient to say that when it comes to Muslim's murdering, discernment is not part and parcel of their agenda. The historical record and the academic voice would explicate it rather differently. After one of his numerous skirmishes, Muhammad illustrates the murdering menace that Muslims are. After the slaughter of Banu Qurayza, a tribe of Jews; the "Prophet" nonchalantly beheaded a Jewish Elder and takes for himself the man's wife, who is named Khadija. Before the blood of her husband had gone cold, Muhammad wastes no time in violating and raping the Jewess. One scholar, Dr. D. Wood, intimates that this bloodbath served as a catalyst and acted as a torch for lighting modern day Muslim hatred, which is for Jews primarily and everyone else generally.

Let us take the lid off this account so we can clearly view inside. Two young Pakistani men carrying knives and under the cover of a cloudy darkness left their own house to go to another. They moved cautiously along the storm drains and culverts that ran along the road side. The only sound was the distant wildlife and so they climbed up on to the road and ran to the gate on the side of the house. One of them had a key which turned the flimsy lock and allowed them to stealthily sweep inside. Their sudden entrance alarmed the lady and she frantically began to repeatedly ask, "Who is it... who is it?" It was of course too late – they were inside. Both men took their knives and began slashing and stabbing the woman randomly and repeatedly, over one hundred times. The blood was daubed on all four walls including the ceiling. But why such savagery? What had this lone lady done to provoke this measure of brutality? The two Muslim "men," in the name of "The Bloody Religion of Peace," had butchered their own mother. They sadistically killed her and it was simply because she had remarried an apostate. Islam and Allah approve the death penalty for apostasy. It is nothing short of ironic that a pariah state like Pakistan which is staunchly Islamic should have so many apostates. We learn from Pew Research that there are more apostates in this "religion" than any other in Pakistan.

If one is seriously looking for the truth about Islam, there are three areas to avoid like the proverbial plague. The first is the press, second is politicians and third are Muslim's. George Bush is still banging the same drum he did a decade ago when the President said; "Islam is a religion of piece." Mr. Bush clearly lives in a cave and has spent 10 years unconscious and unaware of all the murder, mayhem and massacres perpetrated by the "religion of piece." Tragically, the political blue-bloods are all singing the same lullaby as Bush. The press is meant to report the news and not to make it. Journalist's lie through their teeth just to grab some glory through a specious story. One of the capital culprits in the west is undoubtedly the The Mail. It is a right wing mud-slinging and headline-grabbing tabloid. The press and politicians feed us an unhealthy diet of additives and the result is we believe a wrongly assuaged view that Islam is a "religion of peace." Another matter to mention about Muslim's is this word "truth." Whenever one is digging and delving to excavate the truth it is importunate to avoid any fallacious sources such as Islamic. We can, with very little effort; elicit that Islamic ideology is predisposed to dishonesty. When a Muslim is in dialogue with a non-Muslim, the ethical gloves are taken off. Uppermost in his mind is the fact that Islam imperiously advocates *taqqiya* (lying); a licence and liberty to lie for the sake of Allah. If their god exhorts Muslim's to lie it's only reasonable to assume that Allah also lies. For instance, if we ask a Muslim, "Tell me why Muhammad was poisoned by his wife?" The rehearsed reply is that Muhammad died from fever and not poison. Is this true? Absolutely not! (Religion of Peace). It is *taqqiya* – more lies! The People Group have evidenced 11,748 people groups in the world today. They have consummated from this conglomeration that there is only one "people group" that has turned the art of lying in to a science of precision. It is of course, "The Bloody Religion of Peace."

All three agencies, press, politicians and police are inveterate liars and enemies of the truth. For the determined and discerning person who is courting the facts about Islam, then any search must be far and wide; certainly much further than the Quran. Many people are found debating and disagreeing who is the true Muslim. Thanks to the elites, who have taken their pot of paint and whitewashed everything, we are left fumbling for the truth. From Afghanistan to America and Australia you will hear it being said, "Islam is a religion of peace." Now this is an unprecedented statement that rivals Obama's denial of being a homosexual Muslim. Larry Sinclair makes compelling reading and he exposes Qbama's lying lips and lack of truth. Returning to the religion of peace affair, we first need to know who is the true Muslim? This rather simple question has an equally simple answer. There is only one kind of Muslim but luke-warm and half-baked governments have succeeded in causing a cacophony of confusion. The evidence that nails the answer to the question is found in the Quran where true and false blithely co-exist. A glance at Sura 9 and related passages spells-out the "true believer" as one who religiously and ruthlessly follows Muhammad's model and commits Allah's Jihad. In stark contrast, the false and apostate Muslim, may accept the presence of Allah, Muhammad and Jihad but he does not practice them.

When we pause to consider the proliferation of Sharia Law in the U.K and U.S. our response is immediately disconcerting. From Fleet Street in London to Wall Street in New York, Islamic expansionism grieves the spirit of indigenous man. The fact that imams in Mosques rival Pastors in church, which was once an unthinkable thought; is now a chilling reality. Muslims are pro-actively evangelising on the High Street and are converting empty church buildings into ready-made Mosques. What is sickening is that many places of worship are sold for a pittance and in some cases the denominations have naively given them to Muslim's as a gift. One architecturally appealing church building in a city centre with a seating capacity of 550 and was once full; has now become a rattling relic. Whether the Lord left the people or the people left the Lord is still a matter of conjecture. One thing that is unequivocal is that an empty church does not attract people and so it was placed on the market for sale. The church in question was a large two storey structure and was conservatively valued at $500,000. No-one expected a rush; or a race to the church door, but to everyone's surprise there was a "cash" buyer. Mr. Ahmed aI-Muslim pleaded poverty and sweet-talked the church in to parting with the building for $50,000! The buyer reassured the church trustees it was for a noble cause and would be used by "religious" people. We wish we could say this was a rare event but sadly it is becoming an increasingly common occurrence.

Before the paint was dry the former church had invited a controversial and puissant *Shaykh* (Islamic Scholar) to conduct a "religious" ritual in the Mosque. Was it to be a wedding? No. Maybe it was a funeral? No. It was neither of those. The reason for the appearance of this pompous and "pious" man was for one single reason and you may have guessed it. Sharia! Poignantly, it was another Sharia or Islamic law court, which was the very last thing that the country needed. What we are doing says Dr. Daniel Pipes, "Is to make a succession of concessions." Every time Islam seeks an inch of territory we willingly give them a mile. This one seed like so many others, will proceed to produce acres of bad fruit. With numerous Sharia courts being spread across America and Britain like fertiliser spread across a farmer's field; the future is far from certain. British Muslims are now exacting that British law be superseded by Sharia law. They have remonstrated and huffed and puffed, insisting that where the London-Leeds-Leicester triangle exists, Sharia should be equitably established.

What is occurring in Europe is that there is a deliberate denial by politicians and a dismal dishonesty in the press. Many politicians are disingenuous and have lost the ability to blush. Muslim's are steering a course toward the Islamisation of not just a country but an entire continent, and what are the political elites doing? They are sitting in Starbucks slurping cups of cold coffee and oblivious to the lateness of the hour. The "freedom of the press" was intended to allow journalists to report the news as it occurs and not to tranquillise its readers. Those who are judicious in their reporting are the most dishonest. The press make the mistake of writing what they think their readers want to hear, when it ought to be what they need to hear. A controvertible journalist named Katie Hopkins, rightly says, in respect of Islam; "Much of the Muslim narrative is permitted to fly under the media radar and remain there to gather dust." The last place to seek the truth about flagitious Islam is the dubious media. The man and woman on the street, are by and large, ignorant concerning Islam's aggressive agenda. We find that the Bible informs us, "How long, foolish ones, will you love ignorance? How long......will you hate knowledge" (Proverbs 1:22). The public are ignorant due to a concerted effort to suppress knowledge. Parliament peddles a politically correct curriculum that has a loaded vocabulary beginning with Islamophobe! If one dares to say anything remotely controversial about the intrusion and Islamisation of your country, then someone will soon spit, "You filthy bigoted racist!" What is happening across Europe is that the establishment and intelligentsia is sacrificing freedom on the altar of political correctness. It was David Livingstone who made this citation, "When we sacrifice our freedoms; when we give them up they are seldom regained." At the moment Islam has cunningly learned to capitalise on our sense of decency. It matters not whether we comment, complain or criticise Islam, for the response is a carbon copy. Islam responds with a politically correct diatribe; designed to close our mouths and button our lips.

A "Palestinian" Muslima proudly addresses her expectant audience. They listen attentively to her story but are unable to contain their outbursts of exuberance. This woman lives in what is called by Muslims, the "West Bank." She and her 10 children have chosen to live there for the last twenty years. While she gave birth to ten children there are only 7 now. Each one of the other three all died as so-called suicide bombers (*shaheed*), which is not just approved but applauded by every Muslim. Sickeningly, the mother proposes sending the other seven to the same gruesome fate, shallow grave and eternal darkness. Martyrdom for the Muslim is the highest accolade. In the U.K. and the U.S.A, we have posthumous medals for acts of bravery but in Islam you are rewarded for deeds of cowardice. Hammas and Hezbollah actually pay the family of a "martyr" from Palestine a pension of some $50 a month. Not for the first or the last time, "The Bloody Religion of Peace" betray their fixation and fascination with death. As Hopkins accurately indicated earlier, this macabre report went flying under the media radar where it sat virtually unnoticed.

If you have been deluded you will believe that Islam is an Abrahamic monotheistic religion which professes that there is only one and incomparable god (Allah) and that Muhammad is his last messenger. Those who believe that, says writer Elliot James, "Are seriously cerebrally challenged." There is a great deal of deceit whenever this subject surfaces. Imam-e-kaaba states quite audaciously that terrorism and extremism have nothing to do with Islam. Interestingly, the influential Imam omits to tell us that Islam is Arabic for "submission" and refers to submitting to Allah and that Jihad is a holy war for Allah against infidels or kaffirs, who are all the unbelievers.

One of the most prominent peculiarities about Islam is the inconsistencies that are found. The Missionary, Bill Nash, makes a case in point. He maintains, as do others, that Islam is possibly the "largest and fastest" growing religion in the world. This view while viable, is not acceptable by all who study and scrutinise Islam. What is unquestionable is that even though the Quran originated in Arabia and was written in Arabic, most Muslims are not Arabs. Today, they are still divided between two major divisions, Sunni and Shia. The divide is respectively 80% and 20%. The schism occurred after Muhammad's death and since then they have been assiduously slaughtering one another without restraint. Only recently a Kabul Shia prayer meeting was devastated by a suicide bomber massacring 41 Muslims as they were on their knees praying. It is incongruous that from this unbridled episode of cowardly carnage that we arrive at the outrageous title of "The Religion of Peace."

What the two sects apparently have in common is the revelations that Allah conveyed to Gabriel and Muhammad over an unbelievable and protracted 23 years duration! One of the integral items divulged were The

Five Pillars of Islam which serve as a predicate for Muslim's to struggle and strive to maintain in absolute obedience:

1. The *shahada* is the testimony of faith; Allah is the only deity for Muslims. Muhammad is the prophet of Allah. This dogma is an uncompromised recitation.
2. Prayer or *salat*. Five ritualistic prayers must occur each and every day without exception or excuse.
3. Giving or *zakat*. This is alms giving where Muslim's historically gave a percentage annually. Fatwa's, Jihad's and martyr's have changed the strategy and frequency of giving.
4. Fasting is *sawn*. This is a time of Ramadan where eating and drinking is forbidden during daylight; for the prolonged period that stretches from dawn until dusk.
5. Pilgrimage is *hajj*. Muslims must make every effort to pilgrimage to Mecca. For practical reasons such as cost and distance, the number of pilgrims are significantly reduced.

According to Musa Abdul-Malik, the acquiescence or compliance of these five pillars of Islam is sufficient to ensure a place in paradise. If paradise depends on simply soliloquising some sentences then we need not lose a wink of sleep. Unfortunately, there is a gaping hole in his theology. Many Muslim's make the recitations insincerely with their mouth but not their heart. This is undoubtedly why Muhammad Jameel Zeeno and others dismiss Abdul-Malik's proposition. For Zeeno and the hard liners, it is not conforming but believing the five pillars that is the currency for paradise. What is disturbing and even distressing is that the Muslim knows no restraint – there is nothing that he will not do to obtain the "heavenly" goal. The following account will produce sufficient light for the reader to see.

To untie some of the Islamic knots that are prevalent today, we must take hold of some truths. There are many who believe Islam is evil but there are only a few who will say it. A lone voice that speaks the truth is not from America or Britain but Holland. Mr. Geert Wilders is an eloquent speaking Dutch politician who is fearless in the face of Islam. He reports that one of the most asked questions today is, "What exactly is Islam?"

Mr. Wilders begins by articulating that "Islam is not a religion," it is a totalitarian ideology." The Dutch Party for Freedom leader goes on to say that Islam simply has religious trappings and is not a true religion. He asserts that Islam has more in common with virulent ideologies such as fascism and communism. When we pause to consider the Quran in its entirety, we are left mortified. Mein Kampf has the unenviable reputation of being possibly the most abominable book in the world but it has a creeping rival which is equally lurid. The Quran is now a stoloniferous second place and closing. We are aghast to find in its pages that they are replete with anti-Semitism, terror, torture, misogeny, murder, immorality, ideology, paedophilia and homophobia. Not entirely surprising but Mein Kampf has been revised and revived by irascible Muslim's. Both the Quran and Mein Kampf are apocryphal books that are increasingly found side by side on a myriad of Muslim book shelves.

Australia is a popular destination for migrants (refugees) and the numbers are causing disquiet to the point of alarm. The husband of one, a Lebanese, is a jihadist and consumed by the thought to kill as many infidels as possible. He wanted the family to learn about, guns, knives, swords so that they could murder many. But there was a problem. His wife was disaffected and had turned her back on Islam's brutality and was now purported to be knocking on the door of apostasy. Her aim was at variance with his of joining the Islamic State and becoming a martyr. The wife's resistance would cost her dearly. The Lebanese man had frequently demonstrated a lack of love for his dear wife. What was about to happen would prove conclusively that he was not a husband but a monster. He decided to butcher her in front of their three children. Police believe the children were made to sit down while he set about the savagery. When she was found she was covered with multiple stabs, slices and cuts stretching from head to toe. In addition to this he beat the infant children black and blue with a milk crate. A police spokesman announced that the children were in the Royal Children's Hospital and the perpetrator was in gaol. This is not some isolated and rare occurrence. This is pure Islam according to the Quran (2:216) and the imams who teach this "The Bloody Religion of Peace." Such behaviour would horrify all of Australia but Islam would be unimpressed.

Caustic Islam is described by Pamela Geller as an "entrenched ideology" and as such it does not allow for the luxury of freedom. If we glanced over the globe at areas where Islam is dominant – we would find a convocation of uncivilised societies. Any proportionate rule of law and order would be nonexistent and there would be an absence of any freedom of speech or freedom of religion. Common decency and democracy would have flown out the window long ago. When someone is imprisoned the first apprehension the prisoner encounters is his grief from a total loss of freedom. From the moment someone becomes imprisoned by Islam, they are overwhelmed by a loss of freedom. For the apostate Muslim who has come to his senses and rejects Islam, his departure will be expensive – the cost is invariably his life. You can join and leave Judaism and Christianity but heaven help you if you attempt to leave Islam.

Mrs. Theresa May, or "Mullah May," as she has been called by those who have detected her patronising attitude toward Islam. Whenever May has commented on Islamic issues she has always been quite reticent and has never expressed any convincing argument that demonstrates she understands the Quranic ideology. If anything she has been defensive and even dismissive. Several years ago the P.M. did make a speech about ISIS and that succeeded in rousing those M.P's snoring in the back seats of the House of Commons: The P.M. is on record for saying, "This hateful ideology has nothing to do with Islam itself. And it is rejected by the overwhelming majority of Muslims in Britain and around the world." The subsequent diatribe with an irate imam resulted in Mrs. May massaging her message in order to placate and pander to the petulant Muslim imam. Not everyone was appreciative of the Islamic quotation by the P.M. "... let there be no compulsion in religion..." (Al-Baqara 256). If the truth be known more rejected the citation than received it. Some at the conference were clearly miffed that she presented Islamic passages positively but there were some who were furious and for a different reason. What she did was to commit a cardinal sin of seismic proportion. She selected the most benign verse in the whole of the Islamic literature and employed it to subdue the unsuspecting politicians and to butter-up the baying Muslim's.

In 2016, one Christian was martyred every six minutes. Each one had a choice; of a kind, choose Christ or Muhammad. Almost one million Christians were slaughtered like sheep by Muslim's in 2016. Does Mrs. May still believe her speech? "Let there be no compulsion in religion." When all else fails and the plane is crashing: then jump out, with or without a parachute! Allah has included a parachute in his Quran and it is called "abrogation." We are familiar with this ruse. The doctrine of abrogation operates like an annulment in marriage – it cancels out everything that preceded the law of abrogation. What a pity that the P.M. did not read on a couple of verses from which she quoted, and read from Sura 2:258;

> "Allah is the ally of those who believe (Islam). He brings them out of the darkness into the light. And those who disbelieve – their allies are Taught (limits). They take them out of the light in to the darkness. Those are the companions of the Fire; they will abide eternally therein."

It was out of discrepancies and omissions such as those above, that Saddam Hussein chose a phenomenal course of action. He undertook to have the Quran written in his own blood, so that there would be no ambiguity. It was written with 27 litres of blood over a two year period between1990-1992. Hussein sat endlessly with his personal nurse and calligrapher. Since the topple of Saddam and the fall of Iraq the book has been secreted away. There are some individuals such as Sheikh Ahmed al-Samarrai who believe the Islamic work to be priceless but then again there are those who believe it is not worth the scroll it is written on. Not everyone is sold out on the idea of saving Saddam Hussein's bloody book for perverted Islamic progeny or posterity.

One of the many controversial subjects in Islam today is not the authenticity of Hussein's Quran or the implementing of Sharia Law. What really makes waves is the Islamic dress code, namely Hijab, Niqab and Burka. All three items of clothing refer to a general covering of the head. The *Hijab* (barrier) covers the head and neck but not the face. With the *Niqab* (veil), it goes further than the previous one with a veil worn across the face. Of all the modes of dress it is the *Burka* (cloak), which creates the most controversy and there is a good reason why. The entire face and body are shrouded with a narrow mesh slit for sight. As an item of clothing, the Burka is inherently problematic; not only because women wear them to conceal explosives when committing suicide missions but men have also worn them to carry out similar atrocities. Islam sells the uniform garb to disarm public and to tell the tall tale that these items of clothing are symbols of piety and morality, which is of course, pure hogwash. A former Muslima is on record as saying whilst the women wear the Burka to keep up appearances; they dress in western underwear and some women audaciously wear none at all. Perhaps, more importantly, Islamic clothing has been used as a divisive weapon to gain socio-political ground. Once again Islam has seized upon a highly charged topic, which it treacherously uses to cause maximum collateral damage within communities and societies.

Another matter concerns the integration or assimilation of Muslims. It is blatantly clear that Muslims do not wish to be part of a British or American culture. If any one believes that Islamic immigrants come here with the intention of blending in to an established society, they are naïve and foolish. It is immediately apparent that those who come to live in the west have no interest in integrating with the indigenous population but every interest in obtaining what that populace has to offer. All Muslims deliberately maintain a distance and difference, which includes both physical and emotional aberrations. The detailed distinction is not simply nationality or even linguistic. A former Muslim who escaped the ideology of Islam, had this to say, "There is one reason why a Muslim remains isolated and it is because he is a Muslim – all others are nothing more than filthy Infidels." From an Islamic perspective Muslim's are egotistical and self-centred. It is commonly known that the Islamic communities do not contribute to our infrastructure or make investments in our economies. It is highlighted by Jay Smith that Muslim profits go to their home country. Both American and British Mosques pro-actively sponsor terror organisations such as the Muslim Brotherhood and C.A.I.R (Council on American Islamic Relations), Hamas and Hezbollah. It is not coincidental that the last two are listed at the top of Forbes ten richest terror organisations.

The notorious executer, known as the "Butcher," has so far beheaded fifty ISIS men. As extraneous as it appears, Falah Aziz, maintains that "Islam means Peace." This remark is nothing more than another example of a Muslim talking out of both sides of his mouth. The phrase is widely regarded as an Islamist piece of propaganda designed to stop so-called *dhimmis* (non-Muslim subject/slave) from rocking the Islamic boat. Jihad Watch reporter, Christine Wiilliams, dismisses the term as a "meaningless mantra." It should be commonly known by now that this phrase is a hollow expression. "Islam" means "submission" and not peace. Grammatically, Islam and Peace ought not to be found in the same book let alone on the same page. Misguided Muslims are in submission to Allah, Muhammad and the Quran; which in essence means they are indoctrinated or brainwashed. Any freedom a person may have had to even think, has been apprehended and poured down the drain. Islam's interpretation of submission is nothing more than a false facade. The God-fearing American Vice President, Mike Pence, illustrates Islam's so-called submission as a "canary in a cage" or a "prisoner in cell." One could say the canary is free albeit within the confines of his cramped cage. We might also say that a prisoner is free but only within the constraints of his cell. Lastly, a person might argue a Muslim is free but it is a freedom constricted within a coffin-shaped box known as sharia law.

One of the most malevolent sections in Islam's Quran is found in verse 9:5 where it teaches, or rather commands, Muslims to commit mass murder. A particularly venomous verse in the book is 9:29. It is where Allah the Islamic god, orders Muslims to kill the "people of the book." This is a murderous passage that is in essence saying, kill all the Christians and Jews, or the Saturday and Sunday people. Do not forget this is the Islamic "Holy Book." Inside its pages you will find liberty and licence to massacre men, women and children. This reminds us of the words of King Solomon, "There is nothing new under the sun." Nazism was once driven to exterminate the Jews and now Islamism has the same momentum, to annihilate the Jews, Christians and every infidel. What is so repugnant is that Islam's blood-lust is never satisfied. They have an insatiable appetite to spill blood. This absorption with what is grim and that which is gore, is plucked straight out of Islam's Quran.

Islam has been described as an insidious piece of Islamic propaganda that is employed to further the Islamisation of America, Britain and Europe. Sharia in the U.S.A. has penetrated law courts, international media, political arenas, education systems and it continues to proliferate like a malignant tumour. Islamic law's impetus in America is being maintained by the estimated 5-6 million Muslims whose rate of birth is six times faster than the national birthrate of most western nations. It is not unusual for a family to have 10 children. The position in U.K and the rest of Europe is mirrored by the American trend. Population figures for the U.K. are conservatively set at 3.5 million Muhammadan's and in the remainder of Europe, including Turkey; is 45 million (Pew Forum). What is also highly disturbing is the growth in prison populations. An apologetical ministry called "Islamisation of America," report that almost 80% of prisoners who convert to a religion become Muslim's and that over 20% of the entire correction community has succumbed to Islamic ideology. The best selling author Robert Spencer, articulates, "Correction facilities are nothing more than fertile breeding grounds where one Muslim is born every day."

Academic Raymond Ibrahim postulates that if Islam removed the word and practice of "lying," we would witness an overnight sky high increase in morality. A key player in the propaganda contest is Ahmed Bedier. He makes a most telling statement that he may live to regret; "Nothing in our faith says it is OK to kill anyone" (CAIR). This is what his Quran actually says; "Slay the unbelievers wherever ye find them..." (Quran 9:5). We would call such a faux pas as shooting oneself in the foot. American journalist Ann Coulter asks the question, "What one word sums up the character of a modern Muslim?" The answer is obviously "Liar." Advocating lying is not merely an Islamic instruction but a Quranic mandate. The Arabic word, *taqiyya,* is one we have come across before. Muslim's are delighted to use this term since its purpose is to advance the cause of Islam. When we read the Hadith and Sira we elicit no fewer than 15 declarations to lie to non-Muslim's. Such words are seen as offensive weapons in the Islamic arsenal to be used against the unsuspecting Infidel. Choosing to lie has its price. Those who use deception will always be repaid; if not in this life then certainly in the one to come. Many Muslim's lead a life of lies. It is a fact that there are Muslim's who confess with their mouth but do not believe Islam in their hearts. The cost of apostasy is extremely expensive. For anyone leaving Islam it will always cost them more than they have – invariably it will be their life! All four schools (Hanafi, Maliki, Shafi'i and Hanbali) of Islamic jurisprudence are agreed that the penalty for apostasy has one option – it is a dreadful death.

When will European government's act instead of react? Europe is staggering dangerously near the edge of a bottomless pit and the number one concern seems to be the dubious distraction of Climate Change! The West is in the throes of acute cognitive dissonance over Islam and we are worried about the CO_2 emissions from church candles. We have failed to acknowledge that Islamic State (IS) has declared war on us but astonishingly, and the whole of Europe ought to be astounded; we have not declared war on I.S. Can you imagine a burglar saying, "I'm going to rob your house tonight," and you do absolutely nothing. In fact, you even leave the key in the door. This is the crass synopsis being acted out on the western stage between Europe and the I.S. It is utterly ridiculous but this is the farcical scenario that is eked out by almost every country opposing the Caliphate. Unlike its neighbours, Hungary is divided only by the River Danube. The ten million population are all united in their rejection of rabid Islam. Hungary is landlocked by countries who physically fear Islam but the Prime Minister, Victor Orban, is the only leader to speak up. He articulated to European leaders that the problem was "mathematics." "The more migrants we accept – the more terrorism we expect." Orban closed his speech with a rebuke, "Islam is terrorising the West not because it can but because it is allowed." Since hearing his address three other nations responded. Beata Maria Szydlo, the Polish Prime Minister, Kolinda Grabar-Kitarovic of Croatia and the Slovakian leader, Andrej Kiska have forged an alliance against ideological Islam. What is anomalous is the unflinching fact that none of these countries have experienced a terrorist incursion.

Many mistakenly think that two types of Islam or Muslim exist. By this they are not stating the obvious and referring to shiite and sunni Muslim sects. The media also make the same juvenile proposal by selling us we have two forms – moderate and militant Islam. These suggestions fall far short from the truth. There is only one Quran and it has only one Muslim.

Its moniker Islam, or peace, is superlatively misleading. Anyone who takes the time to read the Quran will quickly determine that peace is a fish out of water. The Quran has been called a "manual for war." In one of the 100 or more vicious verses in the book, there is one that declares there will be no Jew or Christian's left in the world. When we glance at the casually laid-back "peaceful" Muslim's in the West, we may be seduced by mixed messages. However, the truth is that these Muslim's are fundamentally no different to their brothers who are waging a bloodthirsty war. The reason most Muslims in the West appear docile is simply tactical. Dr. Daniel Pipes apprises, "This false sense of security that prevails and is conveyed is because Muslim's are presently in the minority and are just biding their time until the wind is in their favour.

True Islam fervently forbids the reading of the Bible and the practising of Christianity. This is the Islam that decrees we all read and learn the Quran. It is Islam that hates progression or anything non-Muslim. This "religion" is materially minded. It wants many things that the West has but it has no time for any people in the West. They celebrate terrorist attacks with singing and dancing in the street. When a Muslim suicide bomber murderously massacred children and teenagers at a music concert in Manchester. Al-Qaeda and ISIS were jubilant. About a week later, on London Bridge, 3 Jihad terrorist's killed 8 and injured 50. Once again, in the West Bank and Gaza Strip, who are occupying Israeli land; there were cheers but no tears.

One of the things that perplexes any discerning person is why Islam denegrates America and its citizen with a passion? Why on earth are Muslim's in such a great hurry to reach a country they detest immensely and speak to a people they utterly despise? In fact, their hatred burns so intensely bitter that they refer to America as the GREAT SATAN? We should not be amazed by this attitude for it is typical Islam to say one thing and do another. We commonly call this hypocrisy. The author Dr. Walden suggests the reason for the status quo; "Islam behave in this manner as they want the best of both worlds." If we cogitate about the logic of Islam; having Muslim's in a hurry to live in the West is as fatuous as a having polar bears living in the jungle. It does not make sense. Islam has a vast amount of experience when it comes to destruction and devastation. Not content with demolishing their "civilisation" they want to export their noxious nature to the West and to leave us suffocating in Islamic toxicity.

It is religious Ramadan (26may-24June) – a time for peace-loving Muslim's to pray and fast (*Sawm*). At the beginning of this "holy month"... 29 Coptic Christian's were murdered by Muslims... Muhammad Mudassir 18, kills his sister because she forbids him marrying her daughter aged 10... In Dafur transit camp 17 women are raped... Seven Jazedi women and children are executed for refusing to provide sex for Islamic State... An Afghan truck bomb decimates 80 and wounds 350... Baghdad bomb slaughters 31 women and children at an ice-cream parlour... A triple suicide bomb in Kabul kills 12 and leaves 90 wounded... Pakistani Muslim gunmen kills two non-Muslim's in shooting... A funeral in Afghanistan sees car bomb kill unaccountable number of mourners... Main refugee camp in Cameroon hit by two child suicide bombers murdering 11 and injuring 33... Russian refugee camp finds 5 year-old boy stabbed to death and sodomised by Muslim refugee... Seven Muslim men rape 10 year old disabled boy in Kuwait... Female suicide bomber in Iraqi market kills 31 and injures 34... Nigerian village struck by two suicide bombers who killed 14 and injured 24... In Somalia 59 massacred with blades and bullets... In Iran government suicide bomber kills 12 and 32 injured. On the very last day of Ramadan; the month that Islam hypocritically reserves as a time of "praying, fasting and blessing;" a most heinous event would scar the human landscape. The fingerprints of the devil could be seen smeared all over this most tragic incident. A Palestinian terrorist, who the press referred to as a "man," surreptitiously made his way to the Jerusalem border crossing. It is our guess that next to no-one have heard of Hadas Malka? At 22 she was in love with Israel, her security work and a special friend. When the light went out Hadas would smile and illuminate the place. The Islamic terrorist approached her from behind and plunged a seven inch blade in to the side of her neck, which came out the other side. She cried and then died. The terrorist was shot dead. "Happy Ramadan!"

"There are some remedies worse than the disease."

– Publilius Syrus

Chapter Five

Sharia

"How dreadful are the curses which Mohammedanism (Islam) lays on its votaries! Besides the fanatical frenzy, which is as dangerous in a man as hydrophobia in a dog, there is this fearful fatalistic apathy."

-Winston Churchill

In the world today we have three score and ten official world leaders. One Head has the unenviable reputation above all others of constantly calling Islam, "The Religion of Peace." What makes this individual a prominent mouthpiece for Islam is his ability to play charades. As a two-term President of the United States it was not until his latter stages of office that he came clean and actually admitted he was a Muslim. Up until then he had lived a lie impersonating a Christian. Many writers had written extensively about his Islamic identity but Brigitte Gabriel was particularly tenacious and eventually exposed him. Being born in to a Muslim family makes one a Muslim and Obama's parents were Kenyan Muslim's. By promoting Islam as peaceful he was not just disingenuous but also deceptive. The former president took a broad brush and painted over anything and everything that challenged him, the colour white. Whenever quizzed or questioned about any matter of Islamic jurisprudence he would invariably back peddle at great speed.

One radioactive subject that was prominent and plagued the president was the polemical Sharia law. Much energy was expended by him in avoiding this thorny matter. Divine law or, *Sharia* (the way) is exclusively Islam's canon of law. It is a legal system with elasticity to stretch to political, social, moral and religious areas of every day life. The Sharia emanated from the *Sunnah*; Muhammad's way of life as laid down in the *Hadith* or traditions. While some Muslims are known to cherry pick from the Sharia; the Quran (33:21) vehemently forbids any prejudicial treatment. In fact, it is emphatically opposed to Muslim's being selective or showing favour when dispensing the law of Sharia. Similarly, any government that circumscribes god's law in any form is counted as a hostile enemy of Allah. Any nation that restricts god's law in any aspect is deemed as opposed to the will of god. The implementation of Sharia is the fundamental empirical goal of every Islamic terrorist faction. As soon as an Islamic province is established, the Quran (9:29) and Sharia (9.8) compel Muslim's to fight against Christians and Jews and all who resist attempts to convert them. In the U.S.A. and U.K. that may mean as many as 90% (International Religious Freedom) of the populations who may deliberately shun Sharia law and resist Islam.

We have, supposedly, one billion Muslim;s in the world who believe they are free when in actual fact, they are in bondage. Sharia is servitude to a set of abhorrent rules and regulations that are the very antipathy of freedom. Of all the things that Sharia lacks, the most glaring feature is freedom. Islam repudiates any religious freedom; even the freedom of conscience is ridiculed. Unknown to virtually every Muslim, a man or woman under Sharia cannot be blessed. It does not matter how many pilgrimages or prayers he makes, for it is futile. Someone who is cursed cannot conceivably be blessed. William Gladstone's words are abstrusely cutting, "Cursed is a most inauspicious place to be. How wretched it is that multitudes of Muslims have the offer of light but implausibly choose a black hole and darkness." God says, "Light has come in to the world, but people loved darkness instead of light because their deeds were evil" (John 3:19). When presented with light or dark; a Muslim will invariably opt for his devilish desire to dwell in darkness. Cockroaches love and live in the dark but when a light is switched on they will always flee in to the dark. We cannot help but recognise a similarity between the behaviour of a cockroach and the action of a Muslim, who is Sharia compliant. He too loves and lives in the dark.

The media is not as honest as the day is long. It operates much like the Freemasons. In the same way the Mason's have degrees of position; the press has degrees of plausibility. We know that Muslim's and Sharia have a word or weapon called *taqyya* which amounts to "lawful lying." There is not one newspaper either side of the Atlantic that is squeaky clean. On the contrary, most of them have taken a leaf out of the Sharia textbook and used *taqyya*. It is an undeniable fact that the only mass persecution in our time is being downgraded by Islam and smothered by the "enemedia." These recent events below managed to crawl on to the third and fourth page of the tabloid press. A Syrian monastery was ransacked, the monks beheaded and the nuns raped. An ancient church in Iraq was destroyed. The women were spared rape but were shot in the head like the others. In the French foothills sits a retirement home for elderly clergy. Each one was coldly killed where they lay. A Muslim man broke into a home for disabled senior citizens and he raped and sodomised two old men who he left for dead. Why did the media either relegate tor overlook these stories? What is it that has put the fear into men and mice? In a word, "Islamophobia." This word is a contrived misnomer used by Muslim's to silence any criticism by non-Muslims. The media and others fear being labelled Islamophobic and so they walk about on egg shells. Those who perpetrated these offences were all Muslim's belonging to "The Bloody Religion of Peace." The Quran provides their authority and Sharia governs their action.

There is no doubt that the West is set on a suicidal course. Herr Merkel and her Germany are listing heavily to the port side and are in imminent danger of capsizing. On the bridge her radio message to other states is one of bare-faced denial. Lawlessness is on the increase and Police are on the decrease. America and the Gatestone Institute name as many as 40 places prohibited to Germans. The tourist city of Duisburg is now divided by 60,000 marauding Muslims. Governments of today tend to lead from the rear for fear of facing Islam and accusations of bigotry and racism. The number of political people who are prepared to stand up and be counted is contemptible. There is a colossal contradiction taking place and most populations are visually challenged. On the one side there are those who are calling Muslims to integrate, or assimilate, into society. People bend over backwards to accommodate their every whim and of course, the more we give Islam the more they want. The likelihood they might coalesce is as remote as finding an honest Mullah in a mosque. There is a good reason why Muhammadan's will never merge this side of eternity. It is because Quranic dogma malevolently opposes it. The prospect of Muslim's uniting with non-Muslim's is as unlikely as Adolf Eichmann having dinner with Simon Wiesenthal. It is not just that Islam fervidly detests the West. The plain truth is that it is utterly impossible for an uncivilised people like Islam, to homogenise with the civilised West.

If you move in the right circles, such as the Machiavellian Muslim Brotherhood or the capricious CAIR (Council On American-Islamic Relations), you will find ample evidence that mosques are not used but misused by the above. Both of these pro-sharia quangos paint a profound picture of a mosque as an army barracks used for military training and tactics. Mosques are used for anything from housing and hiding wanted terrorists to concealing a cache of weaponry. Whenever the subject of an unscrupulous mosque is ever raised, Minister's or Senator's respond as predictably as the weather, by telling us that mosque's have to comply with legislation and can be inspected at any time. This official statement is cavernous and as empty as the cave at Hira. Recent figures suggest that there are more than 1,750 mosques functioning freely in the U.K. and a conservative 3,186 in the U.S.A. When one stops to consider the covert conduct in the mosque, it must be of prodigious import to any national security; for all mosque's to be systematically and stringently regulated. Those who step out of line can be cautioned, closed and even demolished. We have no doubt whatsoever that numerous mosques are prevaricators and the latest pathetic figures reveal that a paltry 9% of American mosques have received any scrutiny or surveillance and in the U.K the statistics are even more ignominious (Atlasshrugs).

Every honest European nation fully believes that their continent is perilously close to capitulation. Germany and Merkel recklessly opened the door and millions of migrants landed like a plague of locusts and there are more plagues predicted to come. Yet, bemusingly, the number one concern of all the countries, is not terror, but the contentious issue of Global Warming! The West is in the throes of acute cognitive dissonance over Islam. We have failed to acknowledge that the Islamic State (I.S) has declared war on us but astonishingly we have not declared war on I.S. Can you imagine a thief saying, "I'm going to rob your house tonight," and all you do is leave the key in the door. It is completely ludicrous, but this is the scenario being played out in Europe. An unnamed MOD official remarked, "we have a greater fear of being called a racist (Islam is not a race but an ideology) and a bigot, than we do of losing our heads."

It is the law! There is not one country in the world that does not have some semblance of law and order. Tikuna is the largest untouched Amazonian tribe which is replete with laws. In contrast, the smallest tribe consists of one man and even he abides by the rules of the jungle (Survival International). In the U.S.A. Congress is having difficulty keeping up with the epidemic of new felonies. Each time there is another crime committed then a new law has to be instituted. At the moment the running total for the decade is over 4,450 crimes, which theoretically ought to generate the same number of laws but not so. The truth is America has lost count of the exact number of laws it previously had. In the U.K. it is rumoured that the nation is law-abiding, which is both historical and hysterical. Between 1994 and 2014 Brussels intimated that a sagacious 49,699 laws were passed between Britain and the mainland. Andrew Parker (MI5) purported; "The country does not need any more laws. It just needs the people to keep the laws they already have."

Of all the religious teaching in the world, Islam's evil exceeds all others. It needs to be made known that the Allah of Islam today, is not the same pagan god as the pre-Islamic Arabs used to worship. The current Allah is a perverse product of the mind of an egotistical Muhammad. The Muslim Allah and Islam is purely the result of a twisted and fertile imagination of Muhammad. We can say with complete certainty that the Quran was not inspired buy an Arabic deity but came from the ulcerated alter-ego of Muhammad, a so-called prophet. What we discover as we remove the layers of deception is that they are flawed; all have a hair-lined crack that forms an Islamic fissure that permeates the falsehood from Allah to Muhammad. About one billion Muslims (this number is always inflated to around 1.7 billion but this figure includes apostates, so the pragmatic number is reduced) have been beguiled and have swallowed this falsity, that "Islam is something it is not."

For many people the very word Sharia conjures up a repugnant reaction. Even those who know little about it will grimace and immediately associate it with all that is evil. We have to understand that Sharia is pervasive and has the ability to infiltrate all areas of society and it achieves this in the same manner as any virulent bacteria. All of Sharia's laws are embedded and enshrined in "gods law" for eternity. The Sharia emanated from the Sunnah; Muhammad's way of life as laid down in the Hadith or traditions. While some Muslim's choose the choicest portions of Sharia; the Qur'an (33:21) is emphatically opposed to Muslims being jurisdictional and arresting what they find favourable. Similarly, any government that restrains god's law in any form is counted as an enemy of Allah. An administration that restricts god's law in any shape is deemed as Allah's nemesis. The implementation of Sharia is the fundamental empirical goal of every Islamic terrorist faction. As soon as an Islamic province is in place, the Quran (9:29) and Sharia (9.8) compel Muslims to fight against Christians, Jews and any disbeliever who resist attempts to convert them.

Today, Sharia is found in many Muslim countries but not all of them apply Sharia Law, or do it ethically. The severity of its application is not always uniform. Stoning for an offence in one country might be lashing in another. What Sharia Law is becoming is ubiquitous and it is seen intricately woven throughout the fabric of societies from Australia to the Americas. Islamic jurisprudence was first heard when it spilled out of the mouth of Muhammad in the 6-7th century and was called Sunnah, or words and writings. Sharia, like the Quran, that was supposedly dictated to Muhammad, cannot be revised or reformed for any reason. It is literally fixed fast like an anchor. The actual legal system, Sharia Law, is all encompassing. The eminent Jewish neurologist, Rita Levi-Montalcini once described this despotic law, "A debilitating disease such as schizophrenia." It is only the perverse "Religion of Peace" that could conceptualise such a catalogue of cold-blooded criminality. There have always been monsters masquerading as men who have committed the most dastardly and demonic acts ever imaginable. However, when it comes to Islam and Sharia, they stand head and shoulders above all others.

Azaz was a pleasant town in northern in Syria but is now an unrecognisable ruin. Water and food are short and basic daily commodities are scarce. There is little money and only crumbs of bread. When you are hungry for food it becomes a consuming pre-occupation. A young schoolboy stands in the corner of a former grocery shop. He notices all the shelves are empty but lying on the floor is a potato. When no-one is looking he boldly reaches down and hurriedly puts the potato in his pocket. An old man, coming into the shop, catches him red-handed. The boy is immediately tied up, charged and found guilty. Addam is dragged out to the dirty and dusty square reserved for punishments. The crowds of men are already forming. Next, he is wedged into a chair and a rubber tourniquet strap from the inner-tube of a bicycle tyre is tied tightly above the elbow. His hand is then covered in liquid antiseptic that looks more like engine oil. A pair of obese men restrain his arm firmly on the table. The crowd is animated and commences cheering. Then appears "Goliath" the executioner, who pompously struts up to the table. He looks at the frail thief and then at the cleaver. In a flash the metal drops like a guillotine and his hand rolls off the table into a bin. A filthy rag is tied to his stump. There is a perverse sense of excitement seen on the faces of the crowd as they simultaneously shout *Allahu Akbah!* (god is greater). Sharia Law has cost the boy his hand and why? Was it justice for a stolen potato? No! It was to appease "The Bloody Religion of Peace." It was purely to satisfy the sadistic savagery of the Muslim appetite.

In Ethiopia the Bodi tribe hold an annual "obesity" competition. Contestants have to drink copious amounts of blood to gain the maximum amount of weight. The winner is the one who has the biggest belly in the tribe. It is strictly run with nothing but blood and milk being drunk. Those competing cannot leave the village for 6 months and there is to be no sexual or physical activity during the event. Islam and Sharia are related to the Bodi's. They do not only drink blood but also eat the flesh of their slain victims. If there is no law or edict to "legitimise" the affair; a Sharia action with an imam or cleric, will out of the blue, issue a fatwa. This fatwa gives them a green light to indulge in cannibalism. As the pen moves ISIS (I.S) are teaching their fighters to eat their victims. Haras Rafiq of the Quilliam Foundation report that a mother in a Mosul was given the grim choice of being eliminated by sword or eating her child. This despotism could only be born or conceived in the heart of the Religion of Peace.

Some readers may remember the barbarous and brutal burning alive of Muhadh al-Kasasbeh, the Jordanian military pilot. The ingenuity and imagination that was applied to this killing was devilish, even by Islamic State (*Daesh*) standards. Islam jurisprudence forbids immolation in principle but permits it in practice! The picture of the pilot, who was caged like an animal, will undoubtedly never be erased from the minds of some people. He stood in the centre of the cage and then they lit the fuel that was channelled in to the cage. The poor soul was slowly and savagely burned to death. His screaming did not last long as he was soon consumed by the fire that was visibly melting his flesh. What many overlooked and have missed; was the great gathering that came to witness Sharia implemented. As the flames enveloped this wretched man; the crowd started chanting and cheering. The air was filled with the sound of exuberance. There were no tears to be found anywhere. But even when Muhadh had eventually expired and all that remained was embers of bone; those assembled were just as fervent and fanatical as they continually cried "Allahu Akbah." While it was Jihadist's that engineered this monstrous act, it was "The Bloody Religion of Peace" that executed it.

If we thought that Sharia Law was restricted, or in some way geographically challenged; we would be sorely mistaken. Believing such a thing would be tantamount to accepting a perverted jihad propaganda. Strands of Sharia can be found in just about every nation and it has the elasticity to stretch across the globe. The reality is that Islamic law has permeated the very fabric of British and American societies. It has gate-crashed in to social, political, moral, legal and economical jurisdictions. A decade ago the number of Sharia courts in U.K. were still in single figures. Ten years later the number is around 100, which of course is vigorously denied by government secretary Amber Rudd. Most people appear to be either oblivious to its amelioration or, would rather look the other way in the hope it disappears. One of the staunchest opponents of Sharia is the perspicacious Brigitte Gabriel who is a Lebanese Christian. She makes the following observation; "While Sharia Law was arguably conceived in the womb of Islam it was not fully born until the birth of Muhammad." Nations have been caught asleep. It is not a coincidence that I.S. has prospered so greatly. With so many countries slipping on banana skins or sleep walking; we should not be so opprobrious that Islam has gained ground.

There are some essential facts not commonly known. Jihad can be defined as Muslims waging war against non-Muslims. The leader of the I.S, the Caliph, is at liberty to gain control through violence and bloodshed. In addition, he is exempt from the rule of Sharia law, and because he is ring-fenced, he cannot be charged, let alone found guilty. This perverse point is portrayed in the following lascivious depiction. A certain self-appointed rancid Caliph, called Abu Bakr al-Baghdadi, ordered an unknown 14 year old boy to his home. The portly middle-aged slovenly man then took the child and stripped him naked; ripping off all his clothes. The self-righteous Caliph then sodomised him repeatedly and so robustly that the child haemorrhaged. After he had finished he threw the boy out and on the street. Villagers soon discovered that the boy was party to a homosexual act. Stupendously, it was not the Caliph that was summoned but the broken child who was still bleeding and bruised. At sunrise the villagers emerged one by one to form a semi-circle. A shadow from the high rise building blanketed those who had gathered. Next to surface was the "Pharisee;" the hypocrite of hypocrites – the admired and adored Caliph.

A stir on the rooftop caused the crowd to look upwards. Two men were looking over the edge of the building to indicate they were ready. At the bottom of the five flights of stone stairs stood a guard either side of the young boy. Ironically and sickeningly, the sign on the ground floor wall said in Arabic "The Office for Justice." When will we learn that there is no justice in Sharia? The popular punishment for this breach of Sharia is to be executed by being hurled off the top floor to the ground below (Abu Dawud 4462 – The Messenger of Allah). "Whoever you find doing the action of the people of Lot, execute the one who does it and the one to whom it is done." Islamic jurisprudence for all homosexual action is always death. The so-called "holy man" was exonerated by virtue of the fact that he was the Caliph and above the law. If Sharia was proportionate then the Caliph should have been the first to plummet to the ground. Complete obedience to the Caliph is a do or die stipulation. With his arms tied behind his back and his face filled full of fear; the two men struggled to lift him up and coldly throw him over the side. Not content that the child had met a most grisly end, the crowd showered his corpse with rocks. Is it Sharia that produces bloodthirsty brutes, or is is brutes that produces bloodthirsty Sharia?

Sharia's driving force is procured from the heat it generates. It is an accepted fact that this religion, above all, is motivated and mobilised by an egregious blistering temperature. Some religions such as Christianity radiate light and heat but Islam is restricted to generating only heat, which is fuelled from a burning hatred in the heart. The rage within a Muslim against a so-called Infidel, is unrivalled. Everything about this ideologically savage system screams death. Muslims known as I.S. (Islamic State) have no difficulty when it comes to finding an imaginative means of terrorising and executing victims. Some of the more sadistic practices include; slicing off finger tips, drowning, burning, butchering, sexual violence, flogging to death, stoning to death, beheading, amputations, honour killings, acid baths, sawing in half, impaling through the anus, castration and female genitalia mutilation (FGM). Women often fare the worst with ineffable acts of heartless crimes being casually conducted. All of these iniquities and many more, are commonly committed by "The Bloody Religion of Peace." If Allah commands it then Muslim's carry it out.

Scientists talk about the "dark side of the moon" but there is a side of Islam that is far darker than this! Take for instance the plight of women under the yolk of Islam. They are treated like animals and their only status is that they belong, or are owned by a Muslim man. Women are used and abused and have no status whatsoever. The following explication of this

Islamic barbarism is seen in the rape of a young woman. Rhokhshana was an intelligent and pretty 18 year old Afghan accused of having sexual relations with her 23 year old fiancée. It was immediately decided, without discussion, that she should be stoned to death. A hole was hurriedly dug and Rhokhshana was buried up to her chest. As usual, some several hundred perverse men gathered to oversee her slaughter. The Muslim hatred for dogs is common knowledge, particularly since over 100,000 were decimated in the Middle East between 2015-2016. However, the hatred for the young woman far surpasses any enmity toward a pack of dogs. If antipathy had a smell it would be Islamic. The stench from the excited, watching and waiting crowd is nauseating. Piles of stones were now swiftly being placed at a short distance around the hole. Standing at the front, impatiently waiting to throw the first stone, is of all people, her vile father. This is monstrous; her very own father first in line to stone his dear daughter to death, What this does is to confirm the demonic dimension of Islam's Sharia Law. The tenor changes and suddenly the crowd erupt in to a frenzied furore and stones start to rain down. Each stone has to be fist-sized. If too small they will not achieve there aim and if too large the punishment will be over too quickly. Blow after blow and rock after rock, smash in to her face and chest and her sobbing increases. Rokshana is desperate and she knows there are only moments left. *"Rhama, rhama, rhama...* mercy, mercy, mercy..." cries the girl. Allah is said in the Quran to be all merciful but there is none – not even one drop for this pitiful soul. Such savagery serves only to reinforce what former Muslim's say; Sharia is "monstrous and merciless."

If we learn anything about Sharia Law, we find it is the height of indecency. Sharia heavily discriminates with it being women again who suffer the most from this evil. The repugnance of Female Genitalia Mutilation (FGM) is a worldwide phenomenon and is a distinctly Islamic procedure. In the U.K. during the year of 2015, some 5,000 (The Guardian) girls underwent this degenerate practice and were subjected to a cruel and degrading mutilation. There are two key factors that are often overlooked. The first, is that FGM is not a medical necessity. It carries no physical benefit whatsoever. The second matter to mention is that the girls, and it is invariably children who are forcibly made to undergo this excruciating enactment. A World Health Organisation (WHO) report stated that there are four common types of genital mutilation. While this is true, all of them involve some kind of Clitoridectomy. This involves removing part or all of the clitoris and any medical aid or anaesthetic, are merely a distant dream.

Experience has proven that levels of prevalence are always greater where the "Circumciser" is located. For instance, Derby in the UK and Detroit in USA are hot spots for rudimentary circumcision. We will not be surprised to learn that all this is done, not for the the girls well being but entirely for the selfish sexual satisfaction of the man. Uppermost in the mind of those who perform this horrific incision, is the removal of the subjects libido or sexual interest. The petulant thinking behind such barbarism is that it will not only enhance marital fidelity but provide greater sexual gratification for the man. But what is doubly distasteful and highly hideous is the method of FGM. A man acts as he thinks and this is reinforced by the FGM experience. Muslim men demand this abhorrent "routine procedure" for their own personal sexual pleasure. The mutilation is conducted devoid of any sterile surgery or any clinical dressings. You have to keep in mind that this is propagated by heartless and uncivilised Muslim men. A razor blade or pocket knife is commonly used and the pain produced is unequalled. It does not matter which method is used for the trauma is identical. There is great loss of blood and the girl is left exposed to infection. Lastly, of the millions of girls each year that undergo this implacable ordeal; not one girl asks for her clitoris to be mutilated or her vagina to be violated. Not one!

Sharia, sometimes spelled Sharia, is derived directly from Muhammad's mouth. Sharia is stealthily gaining ground with more countries embracing this odious Law. In other countries like Egypt, Jordan, Indonesia, and Malaysia the high growth rate is respectively, 74%, 71%, 72% and 86%, and is still climbing. Of course, other countries have embraced Sharia and they are beginning to expand. Wherever there is a mosque, there will inevitably be an imam and he will have a population of Muslim's who are only too willing to succumb to this scandal termed Sharia. The pressure to religiously comply is great and those who do not are very few and far between. From the moment Muhammad stopped using his sword to stir tea and started to use it to spill blood, there has been an incalculable flood of blood that has flowed like a swollen river about to burst its banks.

The Bloody Religion of Peace

In the 1400 years since the prophet first surfaced, Muslim's have mutilated, massacred and murdered no less than 270,000,000 men, women and children. When we ponder what more modern despots, such as Fascism, Communism, Nazism, Lenism, Stalinism and Maoism, have consummated; we find the total number slaughtered does not come close to the 2.7m people! Muhammad makes modern day monsters appear as angels on the Christmas tree. If each of the many multitudes of deceased lost 4-5 litres of blood, it means that "The Bloody Religion of Peace" has spilled around one billion litres of blood! This quantity of blood would have the capacity to fill "Avalanche Lake," in New York. The perpetrators of all those spine-chilling crimes; had a fear of Allah but they will one day have to stand condemned before the True God. Prayer and pity is available to everyone today, even to the "animal" who recently cut open his wife's stomach to remove the baby. He then proceeded to rape the baby and the mother, with no guilt, shame or remorse.

The total number of Sharia courts over the last 1,400 years since Islam's inception, is indeterminable. We may not know the superficial changes but what we do know is that if there has been any change to Sharia it has been in its nature, becoming more ruthless and radical. The world has become more sophisticated which means the methods of execution have also tended to be more imaginative and innovative. Journalist Zoie Obrien makes an intelligent appraisal when she states there are more "unofficial than there are quasi-official courts." She points out that it is easier to be resurrected than it is to ascertain the exact court numbers in the U.S.A. The big picture which is what governments overlook is that Sharia and F.G.M is a tool, or weapon to advance the cause of Islamisation. Sharia is like an ill-wind that blows no-one any good. It is significant that Sharia uses many words but in actual fact says very little. Inside the Quran and the Islamic abecedary there are around 77,439 words, which is about one tenth of the Holy Bible. Most momentous, says Adnar Oktar, is that the Quran has a measly 14 verses attributed to justice, which is a paltry number compared to the bible's 174.

We inculcate to establish in its rawest form, Sharia simply means the 'way' or the 'path.' Interestingly, the Bible states there is "The Way." This is a classic example of Muhammad coining another Christian term, "I am the way" (John 14:6); when he was with Christian's on their camel caravans. Sharia is a legal system similar to scaffolding in that it props up the ideology around Islam. We presently have a pullulating population of Muslims on both sides of the Atlantic Ocean. What they all have in common is the expedient implementation of Sharia Law. It is essential to understand that Sharia is at the heart of Islamic theology. If one could expunge that heart there would be no theology. It is quintessential for every Islamist to have a heart "transplant." Even though the vast majority of Muslim's are amnesic, or oblivious to this imperative, it does not in any way reduce its eminence. It is the thesis of Dwight Pentecost that every Quranic tractable Muslim has what amounts to spiritual heart disease and without the indispensable spiritual surgery, they will give up the ghost and perish.

We cannot discuss too much the ramifications of Sharia ideology in our civilised society. Sharia is the core component of Islamic creeds and is both pervasive and prevalent today. We mentioned earlier that the source of Sharia flows from three orthodox organisms, the Quran, Hadith and Sunnah. Islam is purported to be a fast growing religion but that statement is dubitable at best. Since Islam is pre-disposed to killing multitudes of Muslim's; making any serious attempt at quantifying the Islamic population is imperviable. It was in 2008 that the U.K. government added yet another mistake to its catalogue. Many nationals were outraged by the politicians who were found sleep walking again. Parliament agreed to establishing "Islamic Courts," which in reality are fully fledged "Sharia Courts;" functioning expeditiously. The gullibility of the British government beggars belief! We believe today; less than 10 years later; a suffusion of hostile Sharia courts are in operation. This "legal" system is completely incompatible with British and American justice and is an object of disdain. Sharia has been described by an ex-Muslim as, "Pure poison."

An example of full-blown Sharia Law in action, is undoubtedly the most productive means of comprehending the absolute savagery. The account is vividly retold by writer and reporter, Norman Byrd. "A young woman from Pakistan was physically attacked before she was sexually assaulted. The "Muslim man" then brutally and repeatedly raped this lady by every conceivable means. One cannot even begin to imagine the depravity of the crime and the perversity of the law that was to follow. The arrogant and unrepentant rapist was deemed not to have committed a crime – it was the woman who was at fault for being in the wrong place at the wrong time. It is only in Sharia that an innocent victim can be ruled as a guilty person. She was found guilty of "adultery" (being raped) and received 100 lashes. As each lash was inflicted the skin was torn and the blood could be seen soaking through her long lemon garment. Her sobs and cries remained muffled but could be heard across the village square. The Arabic scholar Raymond Ibrahim makes the pertinent point, "Sharia is not about executing justice; it is all about inflicting law!" Every man (no women are allowed) in the crowd, chanted in harmony; *Inshallah!* (Allah willing) and *Allahu Akbah!* (god is greater). Justice or torture? The victim becomes the victimised under heartless Sharia savagery.

Of all the religious teaching in the world the evil of Islam and Allah exceeds all the other beliefs coalesced. We must be conscious of the fact; Allah of Islam today, is not the same god as the pre-Islamic Arabs used to worship. The current Allah is a product of the megalomaniac Muhammad. The Muslim Allah and Islam is purely the result of Muhammad's feracious imagination. We can say with complete certainty that the Quran was not inspired by an Arabic deity but through the alter-ego of Muhammad a so-called "messenger" What we discover as we strip away layer after layer is that there is a core strand that ties everything that is Islamic together. The umbilical cord that runs through Islamic jurisprudence, is called a "lie." Up to one billion Muslims have been hoodwinked and have swallowed this aspersion that Allah and Islam is the religion of peace. Even worse, there are countless millions who have also been seduced by the same subterfuge. Who would have ever thought that men would be so fatuous as to call Islam good? Many centuries before Muhammad cut the first tongue out of the first infidel's mouth; God's prophet Isaiah warned a waiting world, "Woe to them who call evil good and good evil" (Isaiah 5:20). Islam would appear to perfectly fit this profile and fulfil that prophecy.

Mosul is not a city you would choose to visit let alone live in. The Islamic State elected to impose a Fatwa (spontaneous Islamic religious ruling) on a group of young harmless people, numbering 38. It was Dr. Thomas Williams who first brought this nightmare of Sharia to our attention. Supreme Sharia Judges gave I.S. the authority to kill 38 school children. In the same way that Hitler's Aktion T4 killed 300,000 disabled children, strenuously followed suit and maliciously murdered 38 infants. We must never forget the dear children but we must always remember Abu Said Aljazrawi who issued the Fatwa and executed the sentence. The depraved nature of Islam cannot be measured by a rule or weighed by a scale. If there is such a thing as pure evil then we are staring it in the face with this appalling account. The children were guilty – guilty of being disabled. This is "The Bloody Religion of Peace" demonstrating its loathsome laws for all to see. The face of Islam is grotesque.

Every word in the Quran is allegedly to have fallen out of the mouth of Muhammad, who then gave it to his "imaginary" Muslim minion AKA Muhammad. Islam is explicit in its teachings; ensuring that every *Sura* (chapter) and *ayat* (verse) is fully inclusive in all passages of violence. For instance; Islam teaches Muslims if they kill, or are killed while serving Allah, or, in other words; when carrying out Jihad, they will be immediately translated to Allah's professed paradise. Islam's "heaven," is to our surprise; reputably filled with an innumerable amount of lascivious virgins. It is rumoured that each Jihad who enters paradise will find not one but seventy two salacious and seductive women waiting for him. As elucidated elsewhere, the Hadith alludes to the fact they will then spend eternity copulating. This carnal promise contains a clause that many miss. To receive your passport to paradise it is necessary for you, to slay an infidel, or be slain by one. Not all conservative scholars agree that 72 virgins will be waiting. It is worth noting that this is a controversial text and may mean "virgins," "raisins" or "angels." As far as the esteemed Ibn Warraq is concerned, the 72 may appertain to food and drink but not salubrious objects of sex.

It does not matter how many times you read the Quran, or how long you linger in the Hadith and Sura; you are always left with the marked impression that this is not a holy book. This conclusion is not based on one's emotional reaction but rather through "factual evidence." It incites

Muslims to murder and then promises them a reward for doing so. The author Dr. Daniel Pipes aptly refers to it as a "Toxic Book." One of the most poisonous portions in the Quran is found in verse 9:5 where it teaches, or rather commands, Muslims to commit mass murder. Perhaps, one of the vilest verses in the Quran is 9:29. Here, Allah the Islamic god, orders Muslims to "kill the people of the book." This is a murderous message that is in essence saying, kill all the Christians and Jews. It is tantamount to liberty and licence to carry out bedlam. This reminds us that there is nothing new. Nazism was once driven to exterminate the Jews and now Allah has adopted the same ethos, to exterminate those of The Book (Jews and Christians) and for good measure, to eradicate every other infidel too.

You may have noticed that Islam is the prime adumbration. It wants the best of both worlds with "peace" and "submission" lying head to toe in the same bed. The intelligentsia and academia constantly feed us food that lacks any substance or nourishment. We are recurrently being spoon fed the same stale story that Islam is a religion of peace. Mullah Ismail Medi unashamedly states, "True Islam is free from anything bad so it must therefore be intrinsically good." There were 11,774 recorded Islamic terror attacks in 2016 which resulted in 28,328 recorded deaths. The number of seriously injured was a sickening 84,321, which forcefully repudiates the false claim that Islam is in any way peaceful. The truth or reality is antithetical.

The same mouths that talk malarkey; say that there are moderate and extreme Muslim's. This supposedly alludes to one being more acceptable than the other. In the context of practical Islam, what does this mean? A helpful definition is provided by Raymond Ibrahim when he says, moderate means "rational and reasonable" and extreme means "excessive or exaggerated." The argument proposed by Christine Williams is a weighty one. She has no hesitation in refuting the absurd suggestion that there are two types of Muslim. This is the millstone around the neck of Theresa May. She will not be dissuaded from believing there are two types of Muslim. Those that divide Muslims into "good citizen's" and "radical extremists" are misconstrued. If a semblance of separation is necessary then we should go no further than "Muslim's" and "Apostates." Without doubt the near one billion population of Islam are naturally divided in to Muslim or Apostate. Clearly, if someone chooses to be an apostate they cease to be a Muslim. This is the kind of convoluted confusion the "enemedia" have propagated and force–fed an unwitting public to swallow. To state that we have two sorts of Muslim is as incongruous as saying tigers have spots and leopards have stripes. The Sharia emanated from the Sunnah; Muhammad's way of life as laid down in the Hadith or traditions. It is a permanent piece of legislature because it was written not in ink but with the blood of killed kaffirs.

Muslims are notoriously disingenuous and deceitful. All those who sanction and support Sharia; have been unknowingly caught in a rat trap. Instead of believing the truth they have swallowed a lie. Since Sharia law is obnoxious, Muslim's will be preferential in what they reveal in aspects of Sharia Law. You will not be told by a Muslim that their "holy book" states, "Slay them wherever you find them" (Quran 4:89). Muslim's are deficient of any conscience, so they will have no qualms about liberally lying. In fact, lying for the sake of Allah is not just expected but is rewarded. We will recall the word for abject lying is *taqiyya* and a corresponding verse announces, "Establish that there are circumstances that can compel a Muslim to "lie" (Quran 17:106). It is a fact that a Muslim will go to great lengths to avoid telling you the truth. Their god, Allah, authorises such despicable behaviour and their "holy book" actually endorses lying. Any discussion in the Quran or in any Islamic literature such as, like *kill the infidel*, is avoided like the plague. In contrast, they will talk until the cows come home about benign subjects as prayer. The psychology of this is to make it appear as if unbelievers are detractors and are simply religious bigots, whose real issue is intolerance and Islamophobia; which is highly comical.

We should know by now that the true Muslim holds a literal interpretation of the Quran – he is religiously and rigorously uncompromising. We should settle it here; there are not two types of Christian and neither are there two types of Muslim. That has been a long held myth of a political convenience. A Muslim is dogmatically meticulous in his application of Islamic texts and Sharia law. The Caliphate, have to lean heavily on the assiduity of the law because they are devoid of any nature of holy spirit. For example, in a devastating verse that applies to apostates, we find: "I will cast terror into the hearts of those who disbelieve. Therefore, strike off their heads." (Quran 8:12). We would not expect any sane or sober soul to interpret this in a religious context but we would be wrong. In Hama province live the Ishmaili's a branch of Shia Islam. These Muslim's dwell on the fringes of Islam in sheltered central Syrian villages. Islamic State despises the Ishmaili's believing them to be apostates. Living near the highway that runs from Damascus to Aleppo, has made the Islamic State attacks on the Ishmaili Muslim's far easier. I.S. recently stormed the villages and went on the rampage slaughtering women and children. At the local hospital Dr. Noufal said there were 57 bodies, which including 11 women and 17 children. The hospital reported that many were decapitated, others had limbs hacked off and some chopped in pieces and thrown in sacks like potatoes. The crime as far as I.S. is concerned, is that they were all apostate and this includes the babies. However, the real criminals in all this were the despicable Islamic State butchers.

We have multitudes of Muslims in the world who believe they are free when in actual fact, they are in bondage. Sharia is servitude to a set of abhorrent rules and regulations that are the antipathy of freedom. Of all the things that Sharia lacks, the most glaring is freedom. Islam rejects religious freedom, freedom of choice and freedom of conscience. A man or woman under Sharia is under a curse. William Gladstone powerfully wrote, "Cursed is a most inauspicious place to be." It is a monumental mistake of massive proportion. Blaise Pascal the 17th century French inventor had a heated argument with an apologetic philosopher which was called "Pascal's Wager." Pascal said, "It is in man's interest to believe that God exists, since the possibility of eternal punishment and burning in hell outweighs any advantage of believing otherwise." We gain no satisfaction in knowing that at least a billion Muslims will not see heaven as God sees it. It is rumoured that only "martyr's" will succour any glory. Instead, masses will find themselves furiously embittered at being shut out of heaven. As we enunciate, vast multitudes of Muslims are climbing over each other only to head in the wrong direction. They are entering through the wide gate via the broad road, which represents the way of the world.

Matthew declares what the way of heaven is, "Enter by the narrow gate for wide is the gate and broad is the way that leads to destruction and only a few find it" (Matthew 7:14).

In the same way the words and actions of Muhammad are known as the *Sunnah* so it is with *Sharia Law*. As a legal system it is all encompassing. While some laws or codes regulate public behaviour, Sharia regulates both private and public order. Of all the laws in the world, Sharia is the most restrictive, intrusive and objectionable. Those that suffer most from its draconian measures are invariably women. Theft, for instance, is rewarded with amputation of the hand. If one criticizes Allah (also known as the Moon God), Quran or Muhammad, then the punishment is strictly death. Should a Muslim turn his back on Islam and become apostate or a non – Muslim, the death penalty also applies. A Muslim woman who marries a man that is not a Muslim will receive the severest sequestration, that being death by stoning. As repugnant as the death penalty is, trying to escape its clutches and flee from the consequences, is inexcutable. Muslim's derive enormous delectation from every agonising death.

If you were not aware before you most certainly will now. Sharia is the renowned law of ideological Islam. It is a legal system that has tentacles like an octopus that stretches to political, social, moral or religious areas which are all enshrined in god's law. The Sharia emerged courtesy of Muhammad's way of life as laid down in the Hadith or traditions. While some Muslims are known to be selective with Sharia; the Quran (33:21) fiercely forbids this. In fact, it is emphatically opposed to Muslim's being partial or showing favour. Similarly, any government that restricts god's law in any form is counted as a enemy of Allah. An administration that tampers with god's law in any manner is deemed as opposed to the will of god. The implementation of Sharia is the fundamental empirical goal of every Islamic terrorist faction. As soon as an Islamic province is established, the Quran (9:29) and Sharia (9.8) compel Muslim's to fight against Christians and Jews and all who resist attempts to convert them. In the U.S.A. and U.K. that may mean up to 90% (International Religious Freedom) who will stonewall Sharia and resist the sword of Islam.

Sharia is the optimum legal system with probes traversing all areas of life from the cradle to the grave, which are all enshrined in god's "holy" law. We have already extrapolated from the Sharia that is derived from the Sunnah; Muhammad's way of life as laid down in the Hadith or traditions. While some Muslims refrain form parts of Sharia; the Quran (33:21) forcefully forbids this. In fact, it is emphatically opposed to Muslim's being selective or showing favour. Like wise, any government that restricts god's law in any form is counted as an alien of Allah and opposed to god's will. The implementation of Sharia is the fundamental empirical goal of every Islamic terrorist faction. As soon as an Islamic province is established, the Quran (9:29) and Sharia (9.8) compel Muslims to fight against Christians and Jews and all who resist attempts to convert them. In the U.S.A. and U.K. that may mean over 90% (International Religious Freedom) who will frustrate Sharia and resist Islam.

It is the belief of Dr. John Morrow; "Muslim's are regarded to be disingenuous and more deceitful than any other people group." A Muslim has the capacity to lie to his mother and not even have any sense of guilt. All those who sanction and support Sharia; have been unknowingly caught in the poacher's snare. Instead of believing the truth they have choked on a lie. Since Sharia is obnoxious, Muslim's are judicious in what they reveal. You will not be told in conversation, "Slay them (infidel) wherever you find them" (Quran 4:89). Muhammadan's do not possess a conscience, so will deliberately discriminate and withhold any passage that is "too revealing". Instead, the Muslim will quote the less harmful and more benign parts, such as the practice of prayer or personal hygiene. The psychology of this is to make it appear as if unbelievers are detractors and are simply religious bigots, whose real issue is intolerance and Islamophobia; which is such a ridiculous proposition that it is preposterous.

It is the law! There is not one country in the world that does not have some kind of legal apparatus. In the U.S.A. Congress is having difficulty keeping up with the epidemic of new crimes. Each time there is a new felony committed by "refugees or migrants," then a new law has to be created. At the moment the running total is over 4,450 crimes (over a decade). The truth is America has lost count of the exact number of laws and the legal system is in disarray. In the U.K. it is rumoured that the nation is law-abiding, which is both historical and hysterical. Since the majority of current laws are blown by an ill-wind from Europe, counting them is as impossible as trying to count the 100 billion stars in the Milky Way. Between 1994 and 2014 Brussels intimated that a sagacious 49,699 laws were passed between Britain and the mainland. If you consider that data disconsolate then consider Germany. In the first quarter of 2016 Merkel's Germany notched up 69,000 new crimes and we can all guess what will happen to them! Like the leader of the country they will all be lost at sea. Of course, having laws is one thing but keeping them is quite another.

In contrast to democracy and civil law, Sharia law is unflinching; being set in the same stone that was cut in the seventh century. Sharia emanates from Muhammad's execrable words which are as we have intimated, known as the Sunnah and the Quran which he is said to have dictated. Although, Sharia law is fixed, or fettered like a goat to a post; there is some degree of latitude called convenience. It is common for clerics or imams to make personal applications of different texts. They are known to take advantage of which way the breeze blows. This system of moving the Sharia goal posts is called *fiqh* (etymology). It will be helpful to educe from the civil, or civilised law; that it appertains to public affairs. That would indicate that religious, military and criminal laws would be dispensed with procedural difference. It may be of benefit to consider Islamic jurisprudence this way. Sharia is the "spiritual" law and "fiqh" is a Muslim's interpretation of that law. The pitfalls are blatantly obvious.

This virulent Islamic law known as Sharia, is not immutable. There are fluid boundaries when it comes to guilt, charge, sentence and the application of punishments; which are as long as they are wide. Theft is a crime that merits amputation and the punishment is not carried out in a sterile and surgical fashion but is crudely chopped off as if it were leg of pork in the abattoir. Since there is a profusion of men and women with double and triple amputations, this punishment is clearly an ineffective deterrent against stealing. The treatment of women is dreadful at best and this is reflected in the Sharia. We find that women can have only one husband but a husband may have four wives. Any breach of this law can result in a hundred lashes which will strip the flesh from the bone. At the other end of the Sharia scale the transgressions demanding the death penalty are heavily weighted in favour of public execution. Any criticism of Allah, Muhammad or Quran, immediately invokes capital punishment. The modus operandi of execution appears limitless. The principal consideration appears to be the more grotesque and gruesome the ordeal the more approval the spectators voice. It is by design and not by chance that Islam is known as "The Blood Religion of Peace".

Sharia law is at best an insidious piece of Islamic propaganda that is employed to further the Islamisation of America, Britain and Europe. In the U.S.A. Sharia has penetrated law courts, international media, political arenas, education systems and it continues to grow like an aggressive malignant tumour. The impetus is being maintained by the estimated six million American Muslims whose rate of birth is six times faster than the national birthrate of most European nations. What is also highly disturbing is the growth in prison populations. A apologetical ministry called Islamisation of America, report that almost 80% of prisoners who convert to a religion become Muslim's and that over 20% of the entire correction community has ardently succumbed to Sharia jurisprudence. What is more worrying is that the guards are becoming influenced and sympathetic to Islam.

When we pause to consider the proliferation of Sharia in the U.K, our response is immediately sobering. The fact that imams in Mosques are now comparable to full-time Pastors in church; would once have been unthinkable thought but is now a cold reality. Muslims are pro-actively evangelising on the High Street and are converting all the empty church buildings into ready-made Mosques. What is sickening is that many places of worship are sold for a pittance and in some cases the denominations have given them to Muslims as a gift. One enormous church building in a city centre with a seating capacity of 550 and was once regularly full, has now become a rattling relic. Whether the Lord left the people or the people left the Lord is still a matter of conjecture. One thing that is unequivocal is that an empty church does not attract people and so it was placed for sale. The church was conservatively valued at $500,000. No-one expected a stampede to buy, but to everyone's surprise there was a "cash" buyer. "Mr. Muslim" came forward and pleaded poverty to the church governors. He then perfidiously sweet-talked the church in to accepting $50,000! The imam reassured the church it would be used "religiously" and "righteously."

What is occurring in Europe is a cerebral paralysis with politicians and a dishonesty in the popular press. Many politicians are disingenuous and have lost the sense of shame. Muslim's are steering a course toward the Islamisation of a country but what are the political elites doing? They are sitting in Starbucks slurping cups of cold coffee and oblivious to the lateness of the hour. The "freedom of the press" was simply meant to allow journalists to narrate the news as it transpires and not to sugar-coat columns in order to beguile the readers. Being judicious in one's reporting is dishonest. The press make the faux pas of writing what they think their readers want to know when it ought to be what they need to know. A charismatic journalist, Katie Hopkins, articulates in respect of Islam, "Much of the main material is permitted to go under the radar and remain unreported." China has the unenviable reputation of being the "Fake Capital." However, compared to the fake reporting in the western world, they are like snow white. In mainland U.K. we experience on a daily basis; cases of jihad which include; hit and run, knifing's, kidnaps, child brides, honour killing, female genital mutilation, acid attacks, missing persons, rapes and drug rackets. If we can believe CARM (Christian Apologetic & Research Ministry) and we do, all these incidents are conveniently swept under the press carpet. The man and woman on the street is ignorant of the facts concerning terror and terrorism and it is simply because the press and political elites fear reprisals such a Islamophobe, racist and bigot.

When Sharia encounters a country that is resistant, it has proven adept at infiltrating that society via other means such as the back door. A typical candidate for exploiting would be a country that is politically unstable or militarily vulnerable. The African countries that are economically shaky; have felt the full force of Sharia. Mali for instance, have been plagued by persistent Al-Qaeda incursions. The pattern is predictable; decimate as many as possible and then rape the women and children. There have been two military coups in 2012 and although the political landscape is less inundated there is still a societal insecurity which Al-Qaeda exploits. In countries where secular law and Sharia law operate side by side, Muslims invariably fiercely favour Sharia. Another country that we can consider is Egypt. The Muslim Brotherhood, which is radioactive, have for some years attempted to introduce Sharia but have been frustrated by Egypt's military. Hugh Fitzgerald reminds us that even in Malaysia, Jordan and Indonesia where secular law exists, "The overwhelming majority of 71%, 72% and 86% are Muslim's screaming Sharia and Allahu Akbar."

A so-called pro-Sharia Palestinian Muslima proudly addresses her female animated audience. They listen attentively to her story but are unable to contain their outbursts of excitement. This woman lives with 7 of her 10 children on Israeli land that is Muslims mistakenly call the "Occupied West Bank." The reason there are only 7 children is because 3 have been blown to bits as suicide bombers. When she mentions this everyone vocally approves and applauds. Sickeningly, she proposes to send the other seven to the same bloody fate and dark eternal destination. Martyrdom for the Muslim is the highest accolade. In the U.K. and the U.S.A. We have posthumous medals for acts of bravery but in Islam you are rewarded for acts of cowardice. Hammas and Hezbollah actually pay the family of a "martyr" from "Palestine" a pension of about $1-200 a month. Not for the first or, the last time, "The Bloody Religion of Peace" betray their fixation and fascination with death. Sharia and Jihad are conceitedly charged affairs. Dr. Martyn Lloyd Jones summed them up in this way, "If the lid on the bottle says poison do not expect perfume to pour out." It is worth noting that of the 10 most poisonous sharia terrorist organisations in the world, 9 are Islamic. Hammas and Hezbollah head the trenchant list as the two wealthiest terror groups being sponsored primarily by Qatar, Syria, North Korea and Iran.

"We make war that we may live in peace."

– Aristotle

Chapter Six

Jihad

"Cursed is the most inauspicious place to be. How wretched it is that multitudes of Muslim's have the offer of light but implausibly choose a back hole and darkness."

-Louis Bertrand

It may come as a great surprise that the number of people in love with Islam is beginning to wane. It is as though the tide is turning and the current is starting to trickle out. If it were not for the ebb and flow of Jihad then Islam would have surely become stagnant by now. Sociologist, Thornton, elucidates further with the following annotation: "The legal context for jihad, or struggle, comes from 164 different verses of the Quran that refer to war against non-Muslims (*infidels*). The literal reading of these verses involves military expeditions, physical combat against enemies, and seizing their property to distribute among Muslims as spoils of war. It is these verses, read literally, that license the kidnapping of non-Muslim women for use as slaves in the course of the jihad. It is these verses, taken literally, that commit devout Muslim's to overthrowing any society that does not submit to ruler ship in the name of Allah" (Bruce Thornton).

We must not make the error of viewing the "Religion of Peace" as a common cliche. Islam has been likened to an inflamed volcano. Beneath the surface it rumbles and between each eruption of enmity it convulses lava. There is just one "religion" in the world today that fits this bill. It is only an evil belief system that would incite its followers to burn, bury, boil, stone, massacre, murder, maim, castrate, decapitate, rape, and enslave all those who reject its indoctrination. This so-called "religion" is not Catholicism, Hinduism, Buddhism and is certainly not Christianity. We have only one "religion" on earth that can be described accurately as savage! Idiosyncratically, it has a "god" with eyes, ears and mouth but never sees, hears or speaks. If a pathologist conducted an autopsy on this "god," he would pronounce that the corpse was life extinct. The title of the "god" in question is Allah and the name of the "religion" is Islam.

The Islamic book called the Quran is bulging with brutality. It is imbued with commands and demands for Muslims to engage in a "holy war." Jihad (holy fighting in Allah's name) is ordained for Muslims whether they like it or not (Sura 2216, 9.38). The Quran is emphatic and explicit, compelling Muslims to "kill the unbelievers wherever you find them" (Sura 2.191, 9,5), "strike off their heads" (8.12, 47.4), "make slaves (sex) of their wives and daughters" (Sura 4:24, 33:50) "and continue this Jihad until all opposition ends and all submit to Allah" (Sura 8:39, 9:29). There is a rare animal in Oman called the Caracal Lynx which is unique. All deserts have the same thing in common; an acute water shortage. That means watering holes are priceless. If you are dying of thirst, one drop of water would be more valuable than one ton of gold. When a man stumbles on a pool or puddle of murky water in the desert, the first thing he does is to drink. This is a simple but costly mistake. Most watering places are polluted and even poisoned. The contamination is caused from the remains of rotting carcases that are strewn around the area. Many different animal carcasses can be found in the desert but there is one you will not see and that is the Caracal Lynx. This cat intelligently uses his nose before his mouth! We have every reason to believe that Allah and Muhammad have disregarded the lesson of the Lynx and have been poisoned by drinking from a polluted well.

If you open the pages of the Quran you will see and hear that the prophet is the perfect role model. He sets the height of the bar for Muslims to jump and they do. Muhammad lead by example and waged war, killing, beheading and massacring unbelievers (Banu Qurayza). He made many slaves (Safiya and Rayhana) but by chance did not kill them all. This man's bestiality is unprecedented. He was patently perverted and received a particular sexual satisfaction from young women and children as young as six (his wife Aisha) and even infants to stimulate his perverse sexual desires. It would be a grave error to view this obnoxious behaviour in some sort of historical sense. The truth is that the same sick and sorry practices have never ceased. They are still being played 1400 years later. From Sweden to Spain the current so-called "migration" flood has swept sexual victims aside in its wake. The number is conservatively estimated to be six figures but because of the heart break, fear, shame, and the reluctance of the police, many rape victims remain tight-lipped and silent. However, one subject refused to remain quiet. A woman in her 20's in Norway was cruelly raped to be taught a Jihad lesson. The culprit was her father.

It is highly significant that because of the Jihad mentality and Muslim culture many sexual attacks have occurred in broad daylight in public places. Of course, Muslims take their authority from the Quran (Sura's 4:3; 4:24; 23:1-6;33:50; 70:30); which orders that they take women and children for sexual use and abuse. In Sweden the climate is electric. Native women are buying up stocks of hair dye so they can obfuscate their beautiful blonde identity. Every sexual assault is committed by a so- called "refugee" or "migrant." Recently 4 foreigners who spoke Arabic took a 14 year old girl while she was in school and all four brutally raped her. They then had the temerity to kneel and pray before and after the attack. Then to add insult to injury, they all sodomised her and just for good measure they urinated all over her face. All of this was recorded on their mobile phones. The authorities display a shameful hesitancy when pursuing and arresting the perpetrators. Latest figures suggest a pathetic arrest rate of under 20% and the number of deportations is ridiculously worse at a dire 9%. These disgraceful episodes have been made worse by recalcitrant police forces who are half-hearted and watered-down. The jihad scourge is particularly virulent in both Sweden and Germany. "The Bloody Religion of Peace" has predicated to be bring such countries to its knees by supremacy and subjugation.

Incidents such as above are unfortunately all too common. There is something that sets the Muslim apart from any other being. The anthropologist W. F. Thorpe explicates that human behaviour can be learned or instinctive. When viewing the Islamic context and the Muslim behaviour, he is persuaded that the inhuman behaviour of the Muslim is not learned but instinctive. The following account of jihad profanity is not only unpleasant but despicable. It centres around a Turkish Muslim man who became associated with a young Syrian family. It happened that the Syrians and this Turk were working in the fruit fields of a farm. The temperature was over 40'c so the parents left the one year old under a makeshift sunshade and went to work, believing the man had gone off to pick melons. A little while later the baby started to cry but the parents did not pay much attention. Then the crying turned to screaming and at this point the lone man was seen rushing away from where the baby was lying. As the parents ran over they could see there was a problem. The Turkish "refugee" had tried to brutalise the baby through her vagina but was unsuccessful so he turned to sodomy and violated the poor baby through her rectum. This abhorrent experience was not an event that occurred 1,400 years ago but relatively recently! Implausibly, since the couple were apostate Muslims and regarded as infidel's; the Sharia Court ruled in favour of the Turkish Muslim (Quran 4:3).

Since September 11, 2001 the path has been potholed and problematic. It is noticeable that world leaders are still in utter dismay not knowing which way to turn. Some are oblivious to the fact that there is a storm brewing in Europe named Jihad. Do you remember George Bush who was the former President of the U.S.A? He had a habit of banging the same drum which sounded out that "Islam is Peace." It was not long before we realised he was singing from the wrong hymn book. No one could have imagined that his successor would be a traitor of Judas proportions. We mean of course, the blowhard Barack Hussein Obama. He famously stated, "Islam has a proud tradition of tolerance; Islam is a religion of peace." Wrong! Another former leader of the not so free world is David Cameron of the U.K. His parting words as he left office were, "Islam is a religion of peace. Jihadist's are not Muslims." The former P. M. is out of his depth and his ignorance of Islam is lamentable. The three mediocre men all have a unique commonality in that none of them can see the impending Jihad threat, which is conservatively estimated to be in excess of 25,000 in the

UK alone. Appropriately, the Bible can see in advance what the trio of men could not see in the present. There is an applicable narrative in Scripture that sums the situation up, "Where there is no vision, the people perish" (Proverbs 29:19). Through the short-sightedness of governments and their tepid politicians, people are dying needlessly.

The news today is reported with clockwork predictability. The media appears to blurt out the same announcements about any attack or atrocity by concluding, "the motive is unknown." It is terror related!" Even when the assailant has screamed "Allahu Akbar," (god is greater); slit someone's throat, has an AK47 and explosives; the mendacious "enemedia" pitifully cry, "motive uncertain! Robert Spencer has revealed a sickening report that happened in Australia and received the same insipid press coverage as in the west. This was headlines for a moment and then they moved on to the next new terror attack. Allah says, "Whoever changed his Islamic religion, kill him" (Bukhari 9.84.57). The death penalty for apostasy is a core component of Sharia. This is the law according to all schools of Islamic jurisprudence. A pretty 35 year old happy and healthy hairdresser was murdered not by a stranger but by her "loving" Iranian migrant husband in their Sydney apartment. Murdered seems such an understatement for this grisly crime. In the name of Allah this Muslim man repeatedly stabbed his beautiful wife with her favourite hairdressing scissors. The number of wounds was so abundant that they could not be accurately distinguished. When they had reached 100 gashes they could not go any further and gave up counting. What was Nasrin's crime? Adultery? No! Was she a bad wife? No! Her "capital crime" was that she converted from Islam to Christianity! She heard the words of Jesus say, "Come to Me, all who are weary and heavy laden and I will give you rest" (Matthew 11:28). There are several main methods of leaving Islam and they all require death. One is dying performing Jihad, the second is being murdered for converting from jihad and the last is committing suicide.

We have established when it comes to "religion" and Islam, there is no doubt that the latter is the most bestial and brutal belief system in the history of mankind. It is a fact, says, George Thomas the writer, "Islam's ideology is barbarous and its religion is bogus." There are some 4,300 religions (reference.com) in the world, so finding a defining description for them all is demanding. With regard to Islam, Pamela Geller submits a "devotion to a deity ought to displace dying for a deity." There is a border that separates North Korea from the South and it is called "The Armistice Line." The difference between the two; what separates the northern rogue regime from the south, is the latter is civilised and the former is not. When we consider the line that separates cults like Islam from true religions, we find the antithesis is the truth. Islam does not just expect Muslims to lie. In fact, Allah actually commands them to lie at every opportunity (Quran 16:106; Sahih Bukhari 49:857).

American author Bynum irons out the creases of the Islamic "religion" dichotomy, by declaring Islam as a "system" and religion as an "organism." She intimates that one entity is dead and the other is alive. The so-called Islamic "religion" disputation is best viewed by a metaphorical visit to Pakistan. This country is not normally chosen as a holiday destination and that is because Islam is prevalent and safety is ambivalent. Unlike majestic Kashmir, the southern cities have an unprecedented number of slums and sewers which often accommodates those who are poverty stricken. What many are unaware of is that the duplicitous Jihadist use the same sewers and culverts as pathways for acts of terror. In the capital and adjacent to Quetta Park is an area of pitiable poverty, but it is home to an impoverished hospital for terminally ill patients. On one sun-filled day an event would unfold in such away that it would leave a cloud of horror hanging in the summer air.

On the hospital gate the guard sat beneath the blooming Banyan Tree. A woman unexpectedly sauntered through the gate almost unnoticed and made her way to the hospital doors. Some moments later the guard recognised the "honk – honk" of the only working ambulance for miles. He strolled across the dirt road and lazily lifted the wooden barrier. At almost the same time a young corpulent man entered shuffling his feet and smiling at the gate guard. Several moments later the air was cut by a rip-roaring explosion that devastated the hospital. The Muslim man who had entered was wearing a 30kg vest of explosives under his clothes. He succeeded in massacring 74 men, women and children in the name of Allah the god and Islam the religion. Pieces of body were carpeted all around and all were unrecognisable. The Muslim "martyr" (*Shahid*) suicide bomber had extirpated all the patients and visitors regardless of their religion. Who carried out this cowardly crime and claimed responsibility is as obvious as the moon at night. It was of course the "The Bloody Religion of Peace."

If you combined every evil entity in the world and compared them to Islam there would be no competition. Islam is unique in that it is the only world "religion" that has killed as many people as other religions have converted. It is estimated that there are currently one billion (Pew Research Centre) people with the name Muslim. Unfortunately, we cannot rely on Islamic statistics because many men and women are commonly converted by the sword and since Muslim's casually murder one another, it is essentially impossible to enumerate an exact figure. Without doubt the sheer wickedness of the "religion" and the fact that there is innocent blood on their hands; leaves Islam desperately wanting. In the last generation the estimated known number of innocent people killed via Jihad and in the name of "The Religion of Peace," was in excess of 30,000 (Mark Humphrey's) innocent people. There are of course, many thousands who are unaccounted for with mass graves, incinerators and acid pits; making identification intractable. There remains acres of untold executions but what we do know is that Muhammad, the "prophet" of the Islamic "religion", acted with a seared conscience; butchering and brutalising people, cutting them into pieces, burning and burying them alive. Men and women would be murdered for the most trivial reasons. One particularly profound incident occurred on one of the "prophet's" frequent forays. After one skirmish was over a man remained alive. Muhammad lifted his sword above his head and chopped off his legs and arms, so that only his torso remained. In a perverted way of justifying this monstrous behaviour, Muhammad pointed to Allah and the Quran as his authority and for his supremacy. Muhammad never failed to live up to his reputation as the quintessential psychopath.

The prophet's violent disposition is affirmed by his gruesome record of bloody battles. On the 13th of March, 624, one of the most famous encounters was the Battle of Bad, which occurred in what we now call Saudi Arabia. It was a key battle for Islam and a turning point for Muhammad. It was here that Muhammad from Medina in the south engaged Abu Sufyan in Mecca from the north. The chieftain, Sufyan, was a staunch opponent of Muhammad until his later conversion to Islam. There are traces of this battle in both the Quran and Hadith. Some say it at this point that Muhammad was jettisoned in to the limelight. In the last nine years of his life, and it is comprehensively documented (anc.history); he committed no less than sixty five military campaigns; all in accordance with Allah, the god of the "religion and peace" (Islamic historian Hussain Qureshi). It is notable that the prophet took prisoners for two primary purposes. One, was invariably for sexual perversion and the other for sadistic acts of torture. What is most disturbing is that throughout all his madness and havoc, Muhammad had gained a fearsome reputation for being "merciless." We find the Quran informs us that Allah is "all merciful" but Muhammad definitely disproved that. Throughout his cold-blooded debauchery he used Jihad to justify his sadistic actions. What many fail to comprehend is that Muhammad promoted and pedalled Jihad as warfare wrapped up in virtuosity and religiosity.

Allah appears to have a limitless supply of "blessings" that would wet any Muslim's appetite. It is affirmed that when a Muslim dies during Jihad he is indubitably guaranteed a place in paradise for eternity. Quranic dogma and stark reality are at odds with conflicting opinions over any "guarantee." It is a source of great comfort for a Muslim to dream he is going to paradise when he closes his eyes for the last time. Muhammad believed it was possible to circumvent hell. This tenet is shallow and lacks concrete substance. In essence all this amounts to is just another misleading Muslim myth. We may not be surprised if we learn that there is an inference that this deluded dream is buried in the Quran (19:70, 4:95). This leaves one believing the avoidance of hell is a distinct possibility. The Pope and the Roman church have adopted the same duplicitous diatribe. Every Quran (Sura 69, 84:7) instructs the Muslim to believe that they will go to hell for their sins but after paying a "fine" they are released to enter paradise. There is no mention of the currency for the fine or what happens if you are penniless! The Roman Catholic counterpart would be "purgatory." Nevertheless, Islamic inculcation stipulates the only cast iron surety of being propelled to paradise is through Jihad (Quran 3:169, 9:39). The logic

The Bloody Religion of Peace

behind this ultimatum is debased and deceiving. If a Muslim kills a kaffir in Jihad, the kaffir takes the Muslim's place in hell. Really? No! This is not true but false. It is nothing more than a fanciful fabrication. If the Muslim or Jihadist, dies in the same state in which he lived, then the only possible permanent destination is hell.

When Muhammad died his followers wasted no time in carrying on where he left off, flying the "Jihad flag." Muhammad's favourite daughter was Fatima and she survived the early years, yet is said to have died from the stress of giving birth to her father's child! Yes, you read that correctly. He apparently died six months previously after an incestuous relationship. Incest in the 7th century was endemic and there is little difference in the 21st century; being prevalent and promiscuous amongst many Muslims today. Even now, between Sunni and Shia Muslims, all kinds of sexual deviances occur. Gaza and the West Bank are no strangers to under age sex with Muslim men coveting little boys and girls, incest, female genital mutilation, sodomy, rape, forced marriages, bestiality and adultery all de facto. These grossly repugnant and deeply immoral acts are all currently part and parcel of Islamic "culture."

Fatisma's husband Ali, who was the second convert to Islam, was raised as if he was Muhammad's son. One of the first skirmishes that he fought was against Muhammad's wife, Aisha, who was referred to as the "perfect woman." In less than twenty five years and after all the initial skirmishes, a full-blooded war was waged resulting in the loss of over 10,000 Muslims. It was not a war against a foreign force but a battle amongst themselves – Muslim's massacring Muslim's. No other so-called "religion" in the last 2,000 years, has vented such wrath and shown such savagery as "The Bloody Religion of Peace." What followed was a protracted period of infighting between companions of Muhammad and followers of the Caliph's, who were fervently fighting for the prime positions on the podium. This ferocious power struggle persisted until the Arabian sands were a blood-soaked stain on the landscape.

Muhammad ordered Muslim's to wage war on all other religions and to bring about their submission to Islam. Within in a few decades following the prophet's death, his Arabian companions invaded and conquered the Christians, Jews, Hindus and Buddhists territories. In just less than twenty years after Muhammad's demise, Muslim armies had captured extensive tracts of land and a massive number of people throughout Saudi Arabia. For the next fourteen hundred years Muslim's relentlessly continued their jihad against the neighbouring tribes and religions. In all that time nothing has changed with Muslim's still waging war on a daily basis and people being killed all day long. When one deliberated over this propensity for violence, the only conclusion one can come to is that evil is etched in to their DNA.

If you look around the world today you will find there is just one "religion" with the single minded objective of decimating and dispatching all other religions. It is a blatant and bloody fact that Islam, is the only "religion," who are hell bent on creating carnage amongst other religions. Muhammadan's were actually authorised by Allah to kill with impunity; courtesy of Jihad. Islam has another arrow in its quiver. It is the only "religion" that retains its membership by coercion. Anyone attempting to leave would face the tortuous reality of being killed – often decapitated. Muhammad's mindset was so contorted that he taught that non-Muslim's were sub-human. Infidels or, non-Muslims, were coldly and clinically killed like cattle in a abattoir. Sometimes, they met their end swiftly with a sword on other occasions they were slowly disembowelled with a knife. Unlike today, where Muslim's casually killed Muslim's, in Muhammad's day such action would have been reluctant and met with resistance and eventual retribution.

One of the most disturbing features of Jihad and Allah is the overriding capricious nature. Muhammad was renowned for blowing both hot and cold and so his followers kept a respectable distance. We cannot but notice here that there is a gaping absence of love whenever we read anything connected to Muhammad. Not surprisingly, the name Muhammad and the word love are not concomitant – they are antipodal terms for Muhammadan's. One of the reasons for this is that the theology of the Quran contains more cracks than the Grand canyon. This then leads to crucial questions like, "How can Islam be a religion?" and "Where is the peace in Islam?" These are without doubt two of the most salient questions but they are also two of the most unanswered. Before determining whether Islam is "peace" we must first address the pithy point of whether Islam is a "religion." Myriads of material have been written concerning Islam's peace but in contrast, the corporeality of "religion" has historically been overlooked and understated. General de la Billiere comments, "peace is a mind-set and not the absence of hostility." Is Islam a religion? By any stretch of one's imagination, a "religion" bereft of love, peace and mercy, cannot conceivably be remotely referred to as a religion! If anything it has the character of a sect.

After each of the recent Jihad attacks by Islamic State in America, we repeatedly heard Barack Hussein Obama saying "….those who carried out these attacks do not represent The Religion of Peace." What is worse than him saying this is that people believed it. Some of the population are so gullible that they just simply cannot see the woods for the trees. This and all the other trite statements by the President of the United States are disingenuous and deceptive. Being born into a Muslim family and having a brother, Malik Obama, as a terrorist; would make Mr. Obama's denial of being a Muslim maliciously misleading. Any drops of credibility to comment objectively on Islamic issues have been drained away in Obama's perverse prevarications

The most addressed questions in Obama's term of office was whether Islam is a religion and is it a religion of peace? These two words, religion and peace, are ordinarily inseparable twins but in the Islamic context there compatibility has been surgically separated. What is acutely apparent is the existence of a great division amongst Muslims over even the simplest theological concepts. The words "religion" and "peace" are a case in point. Predictably, if you ask ten Muslims the same doctrinal question, the answers will be manifestly different. For instance; if you ask the topical writer Khwaja Nizami his view of Islam, he will peer at you through his rose coloured glasses and talk incessantly about brotherly love. Another Muslim – Anjem Choudary, who is known for being hydrophobic; has a anarchistic view of Islam that states, "You cannot say "Islam is a religion of peace, because Islam does not mean peace – it means submission." Then there is the pernicious preacher, of Islamic State, Abu Bakr al-Baghdadi, who perpetuates, "Islam never was and never will be a religion of peace." In the "Islamic world" we only have the luxury of residing in one of two houses. One, is the House of Peace called *"Dar El Salem"* and the other, is the House of War, named *"Dar al-Gharb."* Simplified, those that dwell in Dar El Salem are Muslim's under submission of Islam and at peace. Dar al-Gharb, the second, is where infidels or kaffirs are in continuous conflict with Muslims from Dar al-Gharb. Islam's military objective is that through Jihad, there would eventually be only one house – Dar El Salem. The end game is a world entirely of Muslim's.

Naturally, we also have to consider Sharia law and Jihad which are offensive and not defensive institutions. Sharia or Islamic Law, fallaciously means the "path" or the "way" (Sufyan Bin Uzayr). Islam's Sharia is refuted to be god's perfect revealed will. This t*oute de suite* tells us that any infringement is an act of heresy which would lead to a vicious death sentence. We would be short–changing readers if we did not make mention of how unjust Jihad really is. Often mistakenly translated as "holy war" it is in fact a physical "struggling" or striving. Jihad is like a double-edged sword and can relate to struggling to be a better Muslim, which is less likely, or striving against the enemies of Allah, which is more likely. At this juncture there is a clause to consider. Since all non–Muslims are infidels they immediately become enemies of god. We also have the "Hadith" or Muhammad's musings, which is filled full of ambiguity. Of the 36 references to the Hadith, surprisingly only one is pin-pointed to the prophet. The scribe responsible is said to be Caliph Uthman ibn Affan, who was once Muhammad's sure-sworded "secretary."

In the 1950's America had as a president named Dwight Eisenhower who was not only a decorated general but also a formidable politician. That means he could fight his way out of tight corners and talk his way out of trouble. Regrettably, Muslim's have taken a leaf out of Eisenhower book. When we read Bukhari's comments, war and warfare it becomes more transparent (Bukharri 3029). It is extremely frustrating to read a string of Quranic texts, only to discover that before you reach the end, the law of "abrogation" is actuated. Abrogation is a common praxis in Islam and is conveniently used to negate any preceding passages. If we viewed abrogation as an act of infidelity, the other member in the adulterous affair would be "*Taqiyya*" (Quran 16:106). In Jihad jargon taqiyya is "legal lying." We have sampled some of the problematic matters in Jihad, which when collated; reveal a system fatally flawed. Jihad has been bluntly described as traitorous and that is because its author is treacherous. The use of abrogation and taqiyya is extensively reported and regarded by Muslim's as part of their propaganda arsenal and also to contradict the myth about Islam being a religion and peace. We discover that up to 90% the Quran is devoted to unadulterated violence. An Islamic convert to Christianity, Abdullah Sufi, summed up the Quran in two words – "Toxic and Tragic." He explicates that the book is poisonous because the writer who penned it was pernicious.

The Islamic text book also says women, children and disabled must not be harmed but this is one of the apologues found in Sharia's demonic doctrine. We are brutally aware that women and children are casually killed by Islamic State and not one teardrop is shed. It is highly likely that the reader is ignorant of the fate of the disabled and disadvantaged. Those with down syndrome and other disabilities repeatedly fall foul of Sharia Judges. A report by Emma Glanfield opens up a huge crevice that runs through Syria and Iraq like the San Andreas fault line runs 800 miles long and 10 miles deep. The Sharia fault line is of unimaginable proportions. Children, many children of all ages and disabilities are systematically slaughtered. The parallel with Nazism and Islamism is remarkably similar. It was a fatwa issued by Abu Said Aljazrawi that sealed and settled the fate of all such dear children. Incidentally, it was exactly the same evil spirit that drove Adolf Eichmann to throw children head first in to the gas chambers which stood by the burning ovens of Jews.

Fox News (applicable name) recently reported the most horrific story that falls under the auspices of jihad. The incident occurred in Paris and involved a knife man screaming Allahu Akbar (God is greater in Arabic). Typically and pathetically the police say they are uncertain of the motive. Do they think Baptists or Methodists are now crying Allahu Akbar? The victims were the father and brother of the knife attacker. Yes, that is right. The man slit the throats of his own father and brother. "The Bloody Religion of Peace" is uncompromising. Why would someone do something so heartless and horrible? It goes beyond belief. It seems the man was simply doing what the "holy book" (Quran 4:89; 9:11-12) had instructed. As you may have discerned, luxuries like mercy or a second chance are not part of the jihadist's remit. He took the knife to the throat of his father and brother because they were apostate. These two men had seen the light and left Islam. Masses of people are turning their back on Muhammad and their face to the Messiah but it is not without cost.

Many have heard the names Jihad and Sharia but relatively few are aware of the meaning. These are perhaps the two most cogent words in the entire Islamic vocabulary. Islamic jurisprudence purports that it means the "pathway." It is a legal system that can be viewed as a buttress that props up the ideology called the Islam wall. We presently have a threatening population of Muslims on both sides of the Atlantic Ocean. What these two factions have in common is the immediate implementation of Sharia Law through Jihad. Sharia is pulsating and is at the heart of the Islamic ideology that is prevalent today. We repeat for the sake of both the reader and the writer that the source of Sharia flows from three distinct directions; the Qur'an (recitals), Hadith (Muhammad's words and deeds) and Sunnah (Muhammad's traditions). Islam's religiosity is said to be instrumental in attracting would-be followers. It is "rumoured" to be the fastest growing religion and what is significant is that it is inevitably Muslim's who repeatedly make that same empty claim. Ascertaining any kind of reliable statistics from Islam is doubly-difficult since Islam is pre-disposed to randomly killing anyone and everyone on a daily basis.

It was 2008 that the U.K. government made one of its most momentous mistakes. The then Prime Minister, Mr. Cameron, succeeded where multitudes before had failed. He gave Islam the equivalent of a loaded gun. The only possible explanation for such a folly by the P.M. is that he was stewed and not sober. Those politicians with spines, like Baroness Cox, were vociferous in their opposition and animated in their disapproval. However, "Cotton-wool Cameron," now notoriously known for placating every Muslim from Mecca to Manchester; chose to pursue a course that was contrary to many members in parliament and the puerility of his decision would live to haunt him. The unbelievable happened; not in Pakistan but Parliament, where the capital is being commonly called "Londinstan." It was agreed, and far from unanimously, to create five "Islamic Courts" in England. Cameron was caught sleeping. Of all the blunders a Head of State might make this one ranks near the top. On the other side of the coin there was jubilation. This was a sly and slippery move for the Muhammadan's for it meant that those Islamic Courts would be the key to open the doors of many "Sharia Courts." No one in Number Ten knows precisely how many Sharia courts are operating today, but it is reliably believed to be by Pat Condell near 100! in total. Mosques are multi-purpose edifices. Many men and women incorrectly see them as a religious building for exercising their rites and rituals but they are wrong. The picture painted is that a mosque is a camp for the Mujahideen and their myriad of Islamic activities which are mostly subversive and sanguine.

We mentioned elsewhere that mosques are ostensibly barracks that house not only Sharia court rooms but also Jihad fighters. How gullible government's can be. This "legal" system is completely incompatible – it is diametrically opposed to British and American law and is an object of deep disdain. What most fail to see with Sharia is that it is like a disease such as Malaria, that spreads randomly and indiscriminately. One recent case mirrors exactly the unmitigated cruelty of trying and punishing a woman under Sharia. The lady was young and beautiful and a Muslim. Through no fault of her own, she was sexually violated, raped and sodomised. You will begin to understand the perversity of this law when you discover that the jihad rapist was found innocent and the Muslim victim was judged guilty. She was convicted of adultery and received 100 lashes. People have died under lesser sentences and with fewer lashes. When a lash is inflicted the skin is broken and the blood runs. Repeated lashing on the same area reveals the white of the bone, and increases the measure of misery. In between each lash her sobs and cries grew louder and longer. This behaviour is uncivilised and inhuman. All the Islamic leaders present were united in saying that Sharia is Allah's divine will. If this is true, we have to ask ourselves, why are over a billion Muslims following such a merciless monster?

Islam and Allah's evil exceeds the worst of the medieval tortures such as the infamous impalement through the anus. It needs to be made known again in case we are unaware; Allah of Islam today, is not the same god as the pre-Islamic Arabs used to worship. This current Allah is a product of the megalomaniac Muhammad. The Muslim Allah and Islam is purely the result of Muhammad's fertile imagination. We can say with complete certainty that the Quran was not inspired buy an Arabic deity but comes from the alter-ego of Muhammad a so-called prophet. What we discover as we peel back the membranes is that underneath lies a network of propaganda. Islamic doctrine is tied together by a rope of knots called lies. About one billion Muslims are being hoodwinked and have swallowed this deceptive guile that Allah and Islam is the religion of peace. Who would have ever thought that men would corrupt evil in such a fashion that it would appear good? Sententiously, the God of the Bible admonishes the guilty; "And this is the judgement: the light has come in to the world, and people loved the darkness rather than the light because their works were evil" (John 3:19). We have every reason to believe that God of the Bible had Islam in mind when he referred to darkness and evil. The surfeiting subject of bestiality was once an abhorrent practice but not today. Muslims do not only discuss it publicly but even worse they practice it openly. Camels, dogs, ponies, goats, sheep and chickens are all subjected to Islamic bestiality. They have been reduced to calling evil good.

Mosul is not a city you would choose to visit let alone live in. The IS (Islamic State) Jihadist's elected to impose a Fatwa on a group numbering 38 residents. It was Dr. Thomas Williams who drew attention to this and informed the outside world. Sharia judges gave IS Jihadist's the authority to murder – to coldly kill 38 children. In the same way that Hitler's Aktion T4 eliminated over 300,000 disabled children, Islam was emulating them by murdering all 38 disabled children. It is not by coincidence that Islamism and Nazism are concomitant's since both read and recommend Mein Kampf. As the children looked at the jihadist's they shot each child in the face. We must never forget the children and we must always remember Abu Said Aljazrawi, who issued the Fatwa and executed the sentence. Islam continues to show it is cancerous and has been described as a sarcoma by the "The Bloody Religion of Peace."

The Bloody Religion of Peace

Every word found in the Quran is allegedly to have fallen out of the mouth of Allah in to the hand of Muhammad who then gave them to his imaginary Muslim minion AKA Muhammad. Islam is explicit in its teachings; carefully not sparing any sentence or verse that contains gratuitous violence. For instance; Islam inculcates Muslims that if they kill or are killed while serving Allah, or, in other words; when carrying out Jihad, they will be reputedly transferred to Allah's perverse paradise. Islam's "heaven," is to our surprise; suppositionally filled with an innumerable amount of whorish virgins. Even better, so they say, each Jihad who enters paradise will find not one but seventy two voluptuous virgins waiting for him. This reflection is found nowhere in the Quran but suggestions and insinuations can be found in extra-Quranic literature. Those that cross the threshold of "heaven" will spend eternity copulating. However, there is some small print to comprehend first; for this promise contains a clause. To receive your passport to paradise, says Allah; it is necessary for you, the Muslim; to slay and be slain (Quran 9:111). Every Muslim is duty bound to execute their pathological hatred of infidels or kaffir's, by dispatching them expeditionally.

There is a subject that the vast majority of the population are completely ignorant about. It may be through being in the dark but on the other hand it is possibly because of apathy. It is one of the least understood subjects in jihad. We may see a news flash or read a leader in the newspaper but generally the public are clueless. What we must remember at the outset is that there is no depth of depravity to which these savages will not stoop. Most of their crimes are revolting but this one is doubly distasteful. Islamic State has added to its lengthy list of crimes, throwing gays off the roof, decapitating and amputating, child abuse, sodomising men, raping men, women and children and for good measure tearing babies from the womb and raping them. Now the latest atrocity is intended to benefit I.S. fighters on the front line. What they are doing is accosting and kidnapping people on the streets so they can steal the blood from the civilians. Jihad troops are forcing them to give their blood for the wounded I.S. on the battlefield. Jihad fighters have been losing ground and the battle for the city Fallujah has cost I.S. dearly and so they are robbing blood from the local population to give for their soldiers. The unthinkable sting in the tail is that they are leaving people drained of all blood to die a distressing death on the street. All this is consistent with "The Bloody Religion of Peace." After months of fighting the casualties have been mounting up and Christine Williams reports, "Fallujah is Islamic State's stronghold but the bloody battles have cost them more than they can afford.."

There is not one Jihadist that does not seek the death and destruction of the infidel. Every disbeliever is an enemy of Islam and a legitimate target for jihad. It is important to realise that many terrorist groups use the name jihad to wage war in the west but particularly against Israel. An example of an organisation adopting the Jihad position is the al-Qeada remnant, which is also uncommonly known as, "The International Front For Jihad Against Jews." Of course, there are still those among us, who even after all the carnage, perceive Islam as a religion of peace. The former Prime Minister of the U.K. David Cameron, made the insipid comment that, "These terrorist attacks on our country are nothing to do with Islam." This state of denial is not just dangerous but damning. It is rather extraordinary that the man selling newspapers outside parliament is better informed about Islam than the P.M. inside parliament.

Jihadist's are many things but the one thing they cannot claim is to be is normal. Of course, we concede they can be "natural" but we are most certainly assured of their abnormality. Their are two recent events that have caused people around the globe to wretch in utter disgust. Jihad Watch and its overseer Robert Spencer suggests we appraise controversial scholar Reza Aslan. Like all Jihadist's he has a fertile imagination when it comes to the macabre, particularly when Islam is terrorising and torturing infidels. It is rumoured that Aslan is a highly intelligent Iranian man but eating "human brains" must make him strictly stupid. Last year it was reported a fatwa was issued sanctioning the drinking of camel's urine! It was claimed by a crass cleric to be a cogent aphrodisiac and so maniacal Muslims were guzzling camel urine by the bucketful. Not surprisingly, the experience never lived up to expectation, in fact, many Muslim's contracted parasites and urinary infections. The other most recent devilish deed involves Islamic State Jihad Warriors. Many people thought nothing could be more repugnant than using a one year old baby as a suicide bomber but not so. We now have I.S. teaching its Jihad fighters to eat infidels. Yes, cannibalism! "The Bloody Religion of Peace" stoops yet lower. Al-Tabari the Muslim historian reminds his readers by reflecting on the cannibalism that has occurred throughout Islam's history. They even go to the trouble of showing which parts to eat and how to eat them. This is a typical paradigm of Fatwa's of convenience. If it cannot be found in the Quran and Hadith, a cleric can be canvassed to pronounce a "Fatwa" which is a rubber stamp to carry out any recalcitrant activity in the name of Islam.

Continuing with the now global jihad, there is a chilling story emanating from Damascus. A Syrian mother and father have there two daughters 7 and 9, who are sat on their laps. The subject discussed is jihad and the compulsion of every Muslim to perform jihad missions. The girls are told its their duty to be suicide bombers and when they have finished their task they will be in paradise with Allah. If a parent is deluded there is every chance that the young child will also suffer delusions. The father asks the girls where are they going today and they repeat what he said. We are going to be "martyr's" in Damascus city centre. When the daughters ask why they are going to be suicide bombers the mother tells them that you can never be too young to commit jihad. Incomprehensibly, both parents tell their children not to be scared. They omit to describe to them the horror and carnage and instead they firmly reassure the girls it will be very easy and so simple. The girls are kissed goodbye and both of them whimper "Allahu Akbar" or god is greater. Wired and ready the seven year old is told to wander in to a police station. She feigns being lost and needing the toilet. As she walks to the door the suicide bomb explodes by remote control. The result is multiple deaths and massive devastation. It is impossible to identify anyone let alone recognise the small seven year old child.

In Islamic law suicide is forbidden so when we in the West refer to someone as a "suicide bomber" we are technically incorrect. Whilst there is no place in the Quran for suicide there is ample room for a Martyr. In jihad martyrdom, the emphasis is not so much on the person dying in suicide, but on the number of infidels killed in the process. A number of Quranic texts are explicit (4:74; 9.111; 2;207; 61:10-12) and promise rich rewards in paradise such as sex and food. There are many myths about jihad and the main myth is Jihad means a peaceful but powerful battle against sin. However, the truth in Arabic means struggling in the context of a holy war. Those who misread the signs and persist that Jihad is just an inward struggle to be a better Muslim, miss the mark by a mile. Since the old, infirm and disabled (4:95) are exempt jihad, it reveals that jihad is not a course in character building. If it is was genuinely about personal development, why would Muhammad espouse in the Quran references to cutting off limbs and even heads? Let us be totally transparent about jihad. While Jihad may mean different things to different people we cannot escape the fact that it concerns lethal hostilities against the kaffirs or disbelievers.

Jihad is routinely translated as "Holy War" and very often it makes the headlines. For example in 1994 Yasir Arafat while in Johannesburg, called for a jihad to liberate Jerusalem. This was to be a turning point in the peace process. Israel naturally heard his speech and his comments about military means to meet their objective. For the negotiators this was considered as a point of no return in the peace effort and a disconcerting matter for Israel. One thing is certain is that jihad took a seismic shift from then on. Many still remain uncertain about Jihad and one reason is that they do not refer to its source. Jihad as war against "unbelievers" is rooted in the Quran and Hadith (words and deeds of Muhammad). The historian Michael Bonner speaks authoritatively about writers on both side of the divide and reminds us that "Jihad is inextricably tied to violence." When one looks over the shoulder historically, writer's down the ages have spent an inordinate amount of time on jihad in the context of invasions, conquests and today, terrorism. There can be no doubt whatsoever that all classical theologians understand the obligation of jihad to be strictly of a military sense.

The Muslim Brotherhood produces this same kind of propaganda and has an unforgettable motto; "Allah is our objective. The Prophet is our leader. The Quran is our law. Jihad is our way. Dying in the way of Allah is our highest hope. Allahu Akbar." What is so bizarre about this scurrilous organisation is that it is banned in some Arabic states for their malignancy and militancy, yet in the U.S.A and the U.K. they are welcomed with open arms. The Muslim Brotherhood promotes Sharia and presses for Jihad. Formed in 1928 in Egypt it served as a revolutionary fundamentalist movement to restore the caliphate. It has over 80 chapters in different countries, all of them oozing the same pus. They have a global goal to dominate the world and this will be achieved through Jihad and the establishment of Sharia. To achieve their global goal, Hassan Al-Banna their founder says, "The Brotherhood wants America to fall." Another influential villain is Muhammed Badi who has written in the Brotherhood Supreme Guide, "The Brotherhood calls for jihad against "the Muslim's real enemies, not only Israel but also the United States. Waging Jihad against both of these infidels is a commandment of Allah that cannot be degraded.

Gullible governments, and there is no shortage of them; have granted them concessions in status and in purchasing property. In the 1980's M.B. operated with a new face lift and new name called the Muslim Council of Britain (MCB). Not surprisingly, the M.B. spread across the country like a bad breath in an elevator. Their influence spread like tentacles and under the ridiculous title, "Union of Good," raised 50 Islamic Charities, some of which embraced the jihad of Hamas! What all this amounted to was subterfuge by another name. Muslims call it *taqiyya* or lying. It is only the enemy of civilisation that would endorse and employ lying.

A current and long-running jihad is being waged in Sudan. It is without doubt the most gruesome and ghastly example of the evil known as jihad. Working hand in glove with the government, the jihadist's have wreaked havoc amongst the non-Muslims. They have typically killed the men and taken the girls and women for sexual servitude. Those captured are treated worse than animals with beatings, forced marches, slavery, gang rape and genital mutilation. Occasionally, the press find their conscience and report Sudan's state terrorism. The jihadist's have slaughtered in excess of 2 million and displaced twice that number. Islamic academia works overtime attempting to prove that jihad is defensive and not offensive. One look at the Jihad in the Sudanese catastrophe will pull the rug from under the feet of those who are unscrupulous and devious. From the outset and through the course of history, fundamentalist Islam has endeavoured to establish an ontological type of Islam through the vehicle of vicious Jihad terrorism. For many centuries Jihad's have resorted to mass murder, torture, terror, and coerced conversion, all within the confines of its axiological doctrine. This has been the pattern and practice down through the ages. North Korea and Iran have the capacity to initiate a world war but it is Jihad terrorism that is arguably the single most threat to the existing world order. Jihad terror groups like Hamas, Hezbollah, Taliban, Mujahideen, Al Shabaab, Boko Haram, I.S.I.S. Muslim Brotherhood, C.A.I.R. and Al Qqaeda are all certain to do what they can to ensure that Jihad terrorism is promoted and persists until eternity; when all these fractions are guaranteed to meet their ultimate doom.

The recent Jihadi terrorist attacks in Europe and America have proven Jihad's proclivity for terrorist death and destruction. The landscape is changing as the Muslim terrorist's become more mobile and strike further away from the traditional Middle East hotspots. A glance at the map today reveals that Islamist terrorist's are responsible for the loss of many thousands of innocent lives. We may be surprised to learn that in December of 2017 there were 1,137 attacks in the world, resulting in 7,658 fatalities (storymaps). Some diseases do not spread inwardly but outwardly. Jihad terrorism is a malicious disease that advances from the inside out. Contrary to what we are told, it is not shrinking but is growing and poses a severe threat to our democratic civilisation. No country in the world has the luxury of being immune to terrorism. It is not possible to escape the deleterious effects of this widespread scourge. Jihad ideology in its most extreme form is fraught with danger and threatens the stability of the whole world. Quite recently Islamicist's have acquired an influence disproportionate to their numbers. It is a fundamentalism of a special ethnocentric and dangerous form, which is manifested in its tenacity. Of all the totalitarian systems this regime of Jihad terror is perhaps the worst mankind has witnessed.

Jihadi terrorists are irrational, extremely xenophobic, aggressive and blinded by their dogmatic fundamentalism. The basic theme of the Jihadi terrorist is that their vicious and vile acts stem form a heart filled with hatred which is compatible with their belief system. Jihad's think, act and behave differently to those around them. They are avaricious, self-centred, impulsive and calculating, with a total disregard for any one or any thing.

The Bloody Religion of Peace

Whatever their ideology or religious persuasion; Jihad's are cunning, intelligent, self-seeking and sadistic. Their initiative is drawn from the Quran which serves as their source of justification when carrying out atrocities. The Jihadi terrorist is primarily afraid of freethinking, liberty, pluralism and secularism. They are defensive, suspicious, capricious and conditioned by their fanatical archaic dogma. What worries many is that their appears to be no limit to their depth of depravity. If you are doubtful about this, the following account will dismiss any disbelief you are harbouring. Sharmila was a pretty child and very happy living with her family in a village near Colombo, Sri Lanka. This would all change the day she was subjected to a forced marriage. Her husband gained his impudence from reading the Prophet's directive; Muhammad manifested the marriage contract when he married Aisha a child aged 6. (Bukhari Volume 7, Book 62, Number 88).

The nightmare started when the girl was dragged screaming to the local mosque for a forced marriage to Mohammad Imran. Sharmila is merely one of millions of child marriages that are perpetrated by Muslim's masquerading as men. Sadly, she is the subject of a double jeopardy, being murdered and her murderer being freed by the Quran. Seven months ago the child bride gave birth to the first child and is now pregnant again. The little girl was locked in a loveless marriage devoid of any human decency. Mohammed decided the solution to his problem of being tired of his lovely wife, was to tie her to a chair and pour diesel fuel all over this child bride. He then promptly torched Sharmila and stayed until the flames and screams had ended. Islam says she died because she was a disobedient wife and an apostate child. The truth, not surprisingly, is at variance to Islam's "religious" interpretation of this horror story. The official account bares no resemblance to the private ordeal. Sharmila died as the result of being cruelly and callously killed by her wicked "husband." Mohammed Imran claimed he acted in the name of Allah, which is strictly true, but we cannot take away from the fact his behaviour was worse than a savage. If it were not for the trap door of Jihad, his deplorable and despicable conduct would not have gone unpunished.

Allah's Messenger is on record as saying, "War is deceitful." Arrestingly, the Jihad terrorist has succeeded in this strategy of warfare where we have failed. The Islamist learned the lesson of deception a long time ago. Sadly, not only do we not learn our lessons but we are not doing our homework. We have resorted to appeasement and placating the enemy. Politicians still believe in decency, fair play and the white flag. But what do we do to eliminate the predatory offences executed by the Jihadi terrorist phenomenon? Author Dr. Suseelan believes, "Until we stop being indifferent and start being incisive, the way ahead is fraught with fracas." Jihad cannot be won politically since democracy is seen by them as an alien theory. Muslim's are inveterate liars so suggestions of sitting around the table for any dialogue can also be dismissed. Unless we realise that every Jihadi has the same intension – subjugation, we will continue to sink. The objective for all factions in Islam is unanimous – it is not regional supremacy but global power. This amounts to one world under one Caliphate. In the physical realm, it is only by might that these supremacists will be suppressed. Former British P.M. remarked, "The Solution to the Muhammadan terrorist threat is a bullet." Around the globe from New York to New Zealand the same mantra is mouthed about those marauding Muslims waging war on the free world; it is Allahu Akbar."

"Some are born great, some achieve greatness, and some have greatness thrust upon them."

– William Shakespeare

Epilogue

Prophecy - Islam Damned and Doomed

We have in our hands a three-thousand-year-old prophecy which will be fulfilled sooner than later. Asaph was not merely a musician but was also an eminent prophet. We discover this prophecy reveals a climactic, concluding Arab-Israeli war of epic proportions. Prophecy teacher John Valvoord believes the moving of the American embassy from Tel Aviv to Jerusalem will be the straw that breaks the Islamic camel's back. A consensus exists amongst theologians such as Dr Arnold Fruchtenbaum that the Arab nations are those countries immediately surrounding Israel. Significantly, the states opposing Israel have both their ancient and contemporary names enumerated.

Tents of Edom—Palestinians and S. Jordan

Ishmaelites—Saudi Arabia

Moab—Jordan

Tyre and Gebal—N. Lebanon

Assyria—Syria and Iraq

Hagrites—Egyptians

Ammon—Palestinians and N. Jordan

Amalek—Arabs in Sinai

Philistia—Gaza

Tyre—S. Lebanon

The prophet proclaims the conglomerate will include not just Arab nations but also Muslim terrorist factions that have conspired against Israel. Hezbollah in Lebanon and Hamas in Palestine are two notorious conspirators. Humanly speaking, the odds are stacked high against Israel. In the Middle East today, there are a modest 6 million Jews and a mammoth 360 million Arabs surrounding them. It would be wrong to assume that this union of ten alien nations are Israel's only adversaries. Israel has historically and presently had to face a vast number of nefarious enemies.

Asaph had a prodigious position as a prophet for Israel, but he was also a servant of King David. He had the responsibility of writing twelve psalms, but Psalm 83 is most pressing and very pertinent. Arguments exist over the presence of Russia. Dr DeYoung sees one of the ten players as Russia, which is traditionally found in Ezekiel 38. Both Dr John Ankerberg and Dr Chuck Missler disagree with DeYoung on the basis that Psalm 83 and Ezekiel 38 are not the same event but are distinctly different wars.

The Arab confederacy has particular characteristics. They have to come together with one consent (Ps. 83:5), forming a crafty plan against Israel (Ps. 83:3–4), and they intend to take the Promised Land (Ps. 83:12). These fixed features confirm that this is a contemporary conflict. Theologians have come to a consensus that Israel will be attacked by the coalition. However, we are at variance with them, and believe that Israel will not make a retaliatory but a preemptive nuclear strike that will have catastrophic consequences for the Arabs and leave Islam damned and doomed.

Incredibly, Muhammad the pre-eminent fallacious prophet, predicted that Islam would come to a cataclysmic conclusion. Author Nonie Darwish elucidates how ironic it is that a notorious prevaricating prophet should make such an inciteful augury. The Messenger of Allah believed in the future dramatic demise of his bankrupt and inane Islam.

German Arabic academic Hamad Abdel-Samad wrote in his groundbreaking book, "Der Untergang der Islamischen Welt" that the Islamic World would crumble and collapse and the oil fields would run dry. In fact, in a number of Hadith's we find this same end-time scenario for Islam:

> "Belief returns and goes back to Medina like a snake (Sahih Bukhari, 3.30.100).
>
> "Verily, belief goes back to Medina as a snake returns and goes back to its hole (Vol3, Book 30, Number 100, Abu Huraira)
>
> "Muslims will diminish in number and they will go back to where they started (Sunaan Dawud 2.19.3029).

It is tangible from the lips of the prophet, that there would come a time when Islamic apostasy would become pervasive. What Muhammad espoused eschatologically may prove to be the only true prophetic passage that he ever made. The writing is now indelibly written on the wall for Islam, "Chose this day which God you will serve. As for me and my house I shall serve the Lord." (Joshua 24:15).

Biography

> It is in man's interest to believe that God exists, since the possibility of eternal punishment and burning in hell outweighs any advantage of believing otherwise.
>
> —Blaise Pascal

The author has been fortunate enough to travel quite considerably, having visited about half of the 109 countries in the world. Africa is dear to his heart because he worked there a dozen times. He has toured and lived in several Arab states, but Israel has to be the jewel in the crown. Mt Carmel and its vineyards are an awesome sight, and they leave one breathless and speechless. In between serving in the military and working as a missionary, he has attained three honours degrees, which have functioned as stepping stones to writing three books. His home is now in Canada, on Barnstaple Island, where he spends his time chasing salmon in the whirling waters of the famous Fraser River.

Bibliography

Hirsi Ali
Steve Bannon
Louis Bertrand
General de la Billiere
Michael Bonner
Dr. D. Bukay
tom Condell
Ann Coulter
Winston Churchill
Patrick Condell
Nonie Darwish
Dr. William Craig
Hugh Fitgerald
Dr, Arnold Fruchtenbaum
Brigitte Gabriel
Pamela Geller
William Gladstone
Emma Glanfield
Carolin Glick
Elizabeth Goldbaum
Daniel Greenfield
Fethulah Gullen
Abdullah al-Harari
Katie Hopkins
David Horrowitz

Samuel Huntington
Raymond Ibraham
Arthur Jefferey
David Livingstone
Dr. D. M. Lloyd-Jones.
T. E. Lawrence
Ryan Mauro
Robert Morey
Dr. John Morrow
George Patton
Marie le Pen
Melanie Phillips
Dr. Daniel Pipes
Enoch Powell
Dr. J. Dwight Pentecost
Dr. R. Regan
Dr. Bill Salus
Sam Shamoun
Matt Slick
Robert Spencer
J. P. Stanley
Abdullah Sufi
Al Tabari
Bruce Thornton
Dr. Alder Tozer

Rabbi Yitzhak Yosef
George Washington
Ann Waters
Geert Wilders
Max Webber

Christine Williams
Dr. David Woods